Practical Intuition™
IN LOVE

ALSO BY LAURA DAY:

Practical Intuition
Practical Intuition for Success

Practical Intuition™

IN LOVE

*Start a Journey Through Pleasure
to the Love of Your Life*

LAURA DAY

HarperCollins*Publishers*

HarperCollins books may be purchased for educational, business, or sales
promotional use. For information please write: Special Markets Department,
HarperCollins Publishers, Inc., 10 East 53rd Street, New York, NY 10022.

FIRST EDITION

Designed by Helene Wald Berinsky

Library of Congress Cataloging-in-Publication Data

Day, Laura.
    Practical intuition in love : start a journey through pleasure to the love of
    your life / Laura Day.—1st ed.
        p. cm.
    ISBN 0-06-017578-8
    1. Intuition (Psychology)   2. Love.   I. Title.
    BF315.5.D393   1998
    158.2—dc21
98-34520
98 99 00 01 02 ❖/RRD 10 9 8 7 6 5 4 3 2 1

I have been well loved in my life. I dedicate this book to those who love me and those who have loved me and those whom I love and have loved. With love and gratitude. It is my deepest prayer that you know that you have been loved by me.

Love always,
Laura

As always with love to you, my son, Samson
Love,
Mommy

Contents

Who This Book Is For

If you're reading this book, there are three things you should know.

First, it is written for men as well as women. Since there are many possible forms a relationship can take today, and since to address all these possibilities in every sentence would present insurmountable grammatical headaches—she/he, he/she, she/she, he/he—I trust no one will be offended if I adopt the convention that the reader is a female looking for or involved with a male partner.

In doing so, I'm not making any judgments on alternative relationships; I'm simply adopting the most likely scenario among many. I believe that what I have to say applies equally well regardless of your sex or your partner's. Indeed, I am confident that this book will improve your nonromantic friendships, too.

Second, this is a book for anyone interested in either finding a romantic relationship or enhancing an existing one. There will inevitably be some differences in approach, depending on your current situation, so I will address them as they arise. Generally I deal with each topic first from the point of view of someone who is seeking a partner; then I look at the same issue from the perspective of someone who is in a relationship.

If you are in a love relationship—whether you're "just dating," "committed," or even married—the exercises in this book will enhance your understanding of both yourself and your relationship.

Not only will you gain more clarity about yourself and your partner, but you will also become better able to bring positive changes to your relationship in a way that is nourishing and sustaining for both of you. Remember: relationships must be win-win.

While my first book, *Practical Intuition*, concentrated solely on developing the power of your intuition, this one is primarily about love. I will show you how to use your natural intuitive ability as a tool to find and enhance the love in your life. If you haven't read *Practical Intuition*, I'll give you a crash course here in how to use your intuition.

Now, I assume that you are serious about the importance of love in your life, but perhaps you aren't completely sold on intuition. Perhaps the idea seems a little too touchy-feely. I assure you that it is a tangible, practical ability, and one you can develop with practice. And I want to emphasize that we are using intuition only as one tool, and that we will of course be approaching love with our other faculties such as emotions and logic.

So if you're skeptical about intuition, I ask only that for now you try to keep an open mind. If it helps to think of it in this way, remember that scientists have shown that we use less than one-tenth of our cognitive abilities—and intuition taps into a part of that unused capacity. What I call receiving intuitive impressions, other people call "getting vibes." At the very least, the intuitive exercises in this book will make you more aware of yourself and of others.

A Personal Note to the Reader

Dear Reader,

The need to be in a loving relationship with another person is the strongest need that we have. We are either in love, looking for love, denying that we need love, or despairing or fighting despair from the loss of love or lack of love in our life. Whichever condition of love you are living at the moment, your focus is on love.

As it should be. Being in a loving relationship is vital to your health. Babies who are not "loved" fail to thrive; in extreme cases they can even die. And insurance actuarial tables prove it: people in loving relationships live longer. Yet while we are rarely afraid to say that we are hungry or tired or cold, we are skilled at hiding our need for love and often feel exposed when this need is exposed.

This book is a journey to a place where you can have the love you need and deserve. Like all journeys, this one will take some preparation. The exercises in this book take commitment and courage on your part, just as your lover will. This journey may take you a few weeks or perhaps longer, but start it with the determination to complete it. Some steps in this program may take you more time than others, yet each will give you back something that belongs to you.

You have probably read other books on love. This one is different. This time you will not lose your way, because you will have this book as a map and your intuition as your guide to your ability to experience pleasure, to be in love, to be loved, and to find your partner to share your need. You will create from that need a gift that you give one another: love.

Being in love can be a 100 percent experience; don't allow it to be less. I assure you that your lover is waiting.

Our First Experiment

Stop!
Complete This Assignment Before Reading Any Further!

EXERCISE 1: PLEASE YOURSELF

Set aside some time to do something you enjoy. That's right. I simply want you to indulge in a pleasurable activity.

How you do this is up to you. It may mean listening to your favorite music, or getting a foot massage, or getting a foot massage while listening to your favorite music. Again, it's completely up to you.

There are only three requirements for this assignment. First, you must perform it consciously. Dedicate some fixed period in which you are going to luxuriate yourself in pleasure. Set aside at least an hour; an afternoon is even better; a whole day is better still.

Second, during this assignment you are permitted to do only that which gives you pleasure—and nothing else. For its duration, you will be completely self-indulgent.

Third and last, I want you to notice your thoughts, feelings, and other sensations as you experience pleasure. If you want to record your impressions—and you may find doing so worthwhile—wait until the assignment is over.

That's it. Remember: don't read anything else in this book until you complete this assignment. We'll return to discuss it in chapter 1.

Introduction

The Beginning of a Journey

You are about to begin a journey of being "in love" as a way of life. *Practical Intuition™ in Love* will allow you to experience falling in love and being in love, whether or not you have a lover. There are people who naturally attract love to them by first experiencing love within themselves and their lives.

This book will show you how to become one of these people. You'll learn to use your intuition to help you find a lover—if that is what you want—or how to enrich your existing love relationships. You will learn a practical methodology not only for attracting what you want, but also for discovering what it is you want in the first place. This book will enhance your ability to bring pleasure to all of your relationships, while putting the love back into your life and the joy back into the way you love. *Practical Intuition™ in Love* will heighten your perception and experience of pleasure, as well as provide a step-by-step program to attract the love you want, or to transform the love you already have.

A Step-by-Step Program to Find and Enhance Love— Starting Today!

This book answers two simple questions: What are the circumstances that allow us to attract love into our lives? Once we have it, how can we sustain it and make it grow?

You've already started on your journey to love by doing the first assignment at the beginning of this book (which we'll be discussing shortly in the next chapter). I've arranged the journey into an easy-to-follow program of six simple steps. These steps build on one another, so it's important that you work your way through the program in order. They are:

Step One: Finding the State of Pleasure
Step Two: Creating the Map
Step Three: Clearing the Field
Step Four: Finding the Garden of Eden
Step Five: Caring for Your Garden
Step Six: Sharing Your Garden

Keep in mind that these steps often overlap, so it's important to read these chapters and do the exercises in sequence. In Step Two, for example, you'll be establishing your love goal. As you do the exercises in the following steps, however, you will notice that your love goal *changes* in subtle and sometimes surprising ways.

Love in the Popular Press

I'm sure you've seen countless books and articles on finding love. The titles always seem to be variations on the same old themes: *How to Catch the Perfect Guy. The Ultimate Rules for Dating Success. Twenty Sure-Fire Ways to Find and Marry the Mate of Your Dreams.*

A lot of what's written about love focuses on how to catch your partner, how to trick your partner, how to win control over your partner. In a sense, the popular literature reflects what love has become in our society: a hunting game.

Many of these books and articles provide tips and "rules" for playing the love game, though of course these "rules" vary from author to
author. According to one expert on love, women should play hard to
get. Another advises readers to be more accessible and more responsive to their partners' needs. Some teach you how to communicate
better, or negotiate more effectively, or how to use body language that
conveys your availability. The goal always seems to be the same: you
meet a man (or woman); you do whatever it takes to reel him in; and
then you make sure you continually manipulate the situation to keep
the balance of power in your favor.

Some of these methods may work on some people some of the
time, but is this what you really want from your love life? This
approach to finding romance more often resembles war than love.
Such books on love invariably focus on the many differences between
men and women. Yet this approach simply fuels a sense of distrust
between the sexes, which adds to the difficulty of finding a lasting
love relationship. There are of course differences between men and
women. Thank goodness! But to focus on these differences too closely
is not particularly helpful in attracting love to our lives. Indeed, it
might even be counterproductive.

How This Book Is Different

I don't believe in magic formulas. Each person is different; each lover
and each love relationship has its own requirements.

To be truly effective in love—to attract, maintain, and be satisfied
with love—you must see yourself and your lover as unique individuals. This means you must see each other as separate people with
unique needs, desires, points of attraction, areas of insecurity, means
of expression and communicating, and ways of interpreting life.

Love is not about "catching" someone. It is about *beguiling*, a word
I use to describe that first state of mystical pleasure. And it is about
the other kind of love that makes romantic love sustain itself: friendship. Love is an inner state that allows us to see our lives more sympa-
thetically. In a state of love, we recognize or even create possibilities
in the environment where before the terrain was flat. The chemicals

in our body give us a sense of well-being and euphoria. We are kinder to ourselves.

Love also allows us to connect to something else in a profound and life-affirming way. Together we are going to create both in your life. And we'll start by finding out what the state of love is. Then I'll show you how to use all of your resources—with your intuition as a guide—to attract that love into your life *naturally*.

Why Intuition and Love?

Your intuition is a powerful natural ability that operates all the time—it's working right now as you read these words. Intuition is a way of gathering information not immediately present to your senses. It can help you get in touch with your own needs as well as those of your present or future partner. Since intuition can both enhance and interfere with relationships, it's important for you to gain conscious control over its power. I'll show you how to do that shortly. You'll also learn how to use intuition to receive signals from others. You'll learn not only *how* to send signals to others but also *which* ones to send.

Love Is Something to Be Experienced Rather Than Understood

Most profound experiences in life happen without our understanding them at the time. The understanding comes only after the experience. A great philosopher once said that life must be lived forward, but it can be understood only backward. The same is true in love.

This is why I asked you to complete the first exercise, on page xiii, without any explanation. To get the full benefit of this book, you will need to work through many such exercises conscientiously. This shouldn't be difficult, since you will see the benefits almost immediately. Keep the following points in mind:

- Each exercise builds on earlier ones, so please do them in order. Don't be surprised if you find yourself doing exercises that overlap. We will approach each particular issue from several angles to allow you varying perspectives and richer insights.

- Some exercises will ask you to reflect consciously on your thoughts and feelings; others are intuitive in nature. You'll use your intuition to find the answers to questions you don't even know!

- Some exercises may seem silly as you do them; occasionally you won't even know what you're doing until you've completed the exercise. Remember that your needs and feelings are not always obvious, and many are subconscious. We may need to resort to indirect methods to plumb your emotional depths.

- Don't be frustrated if some exercises don't work right away. If you do the exercises with an open mind, each one will spark valuable insights.

- These insights might not occur immediately, so from time to time, look back over your old exercises. Your impressions from an exercise may not make sense today, but they will in time as you progress through the program and gain further awareness of yourself and your needs.

- Finally, if you're currently in a relationship, you may want to work on some exercises with your partner; the choice is up to you—and your partner!

The bottom line is to keep an open mind. As you read this book and follow my program, your life will quickly begin to change. In truth, I am putting forth a whole new concept of love. Try it out. The proof of the pudding is in the eating. By the time you finish, I think you will find that my program works.

Keep a Journal to Record Your Love Journey

If you don't already keep a journal, I strongly urge you to start one now. Throughout history, artists, scientists, and others have found a journal to be an indispensable tool for self-discovery. Keeping one will help you get in touch with your feelings and express them.

You will experience a great deal of personal growth as you work your way through this book. Being able to look back over your earlier work will help you mark your progress. During a time of calm, a journal can also record today's insights on how to deal with tomorrow's potential crisis. These suggestions might be as simple as "When he's talking about freedom he's really feeling unwanted" or "She tends to be most open to hearing constructive criticism when she is eating something she likes."

In choosing a journal, keep the following points in mind:

- I recommend a three-ring binder rather than a bound journal, since you'll probably want to return to previous exercises and add pages. Your journal does not have to be fancy. In fact, the simpler your journal is, the more you can make it your own in creative ways.

- As you work through the program, you may find yourself clipping love images significant to you and forming a collage on the cover. We'll do an exercise devoted to this. Leave the inside back cover free; once you've achieved your love goal, you can acknowledge it visually there.

Working in your journal is therapeutic as well as enlightening. Doing so daily will help you affirm the seriousness of your goal—finding and enhancing the love in your life—especially when you encounter difficult times. I can't tell you how many times people, including myself, have gone back to the pages of their love book during a time of relationship crisis and jogged their memory about why they fell in love with their mate in the first place.

Form a Support Network for Your Love Journey

Some activities—like jogging, for example—are easier to do with a partner. A jogging partner is someone you can talk with as you jog, which helps to pass time that might otherwise be tedious or difficult. Just knowing you have a jogging partner who expects to meet you can make getting out of bed at seven o'clock in the morning easier.

You may find it helpful to form a support group as you work your way through this book. It almost always helps to share your experiences and revelations with someone.

Let's Get Started

In the next six steps, you will be freeing your power to love and to attract love by using your intuition. A fundamental point of this book is that in our single-minded search for love, we too often abandon our friendships and everything else good and pleasurable in our life, and in so doing set ourselves up for failure. So, paradoxically, the first step in finding love is to forget about finding it for a while!

Practical
Intuition™
IN LOVE

STEP ONE

Falling in Love

Love Byte

You Hold the Key to Falling in Love

The process of falling in love begins with an initial attraction between two people. At the very beginning, this is largely a chemical process.

Now, have you ever noticed that as soon as someone falls in love, dozens of other suitors seem to fall out of the trees in pursuit! Isn't it ironic? Perhaps you've even experienced this yourself. Where were they when we were alone?

Paradoxically, the easiest way to find love is to be in love. This sounds like a catch-22: to find love we must be attractive, but we are most attractive when we are in love! The secret to attracting others is not to appear attractive (although that plays a part, of course), but rather to be attractive.

Wouldn't it be great if we could somehow re-create in ourselves the physiological state of love, even if we didn't yet have love in our life? By re-creating the physiological state of love in ourselves, we would naturally become more attractive, since our body's biochemistry can't tell the difference from the real thing.

Well, you can become a "love magnet," drawing compatible partners to you effortlessly. How? Simply by seeking pleasure. Pleasurable activities reproduce virtually the same physiological state we experience when we are in love. The trick is that when we don't have love in our lives, we tend to avoid the very joyous and pleasurable activities that would make us more attractive.

Loving and being in love, then, are natural states. You don't have to do anything to find love. Love will come into your life if you simply remove the obstacles that are standing in its way. And we start the process by creating love not tomorrow but today, right now.

ᘒ 1 ᘒ

Creating the State of Love from the State of Pleasure

Welcome Back: Reviewing Your First Exercise

By now, you've completed the exercise on page xiii. When you began it, the assignment may have seemed easy. What could be simpler? Someone is not only asking me to indulge myself, but insisting on it!

But many people report that the assignment was more difficult than they had imagined. Often people find they don't know how to go about indulging in pleasurable activities without feeling awkward. Others actually report an internal resistance to giving themselves pleasure.

How did you feel? Be honest. Were you self-conscious? Did you feel self-centered? A bit awkward? Guilty? Undeserving? Too depressed to enjoy yourself?

Love and joy are synonymous. The state of love and being in love is one of intense pleasure. Although a love relationship can be an enormous source of pain, the perceptual, physical, emotional, and energetic experience of love itself is the experience of pleasure.

The *Practical Intuition™ in Love* program is not about waiting to find the "perfect" mate or lover, or waiting for your current relationship to improve. It's about learning how to take joy and pleasure in the here and now. Which is another reason why we did the "pleasure experiment" before anything else.

Before Falling in Love, You Must First Fall into a State of Pleasure

Love—chemically, emotionally, and psychically—occurred in you long before you actually arrived at the age of sexual development or met a mate. As a child, you experienced it with your parents, your friends, your toys, your pets, your ideas, your favorite foods or places. You fell in love with things, people, and experiences that brought you comfort and pleasure.

Do you remember when you were a teenager, before you had your first sexual attraction? Your best friend was everything. Or perhaps your dominant relationship was with your teacher, coach, or even a hero in a movie or book, or your plans and dreams. Earlier still it was with your mother or your father or your dog.

When you fall in love, you fall into a state of pleasure. Love is fundamentally about pleasure, both the pleasure we give and the pleasure we receive. Being able to experience pleasure fully is a precondition for falling in love with the right person.

By pleasure I do not mean simply sexual gratification, though sex is of course a very important part of being in love. Love begins when you are able to take pleasure in simple, everyday activities. Love, on a biochemical level, is a heightened sense of pleasure. We form our love relationships for a variety of reasons, but each one should be experienced in a way that increases pleasure in life.

Yet in my practice, I continually come across bad relationships in which partners are making each other's life miserable. Do we eat foods primarily for their nutritional content or for the pleasure they bring us? If you don't really like broccoli, do you force yourself to eat it—or do you try to change the experience of eating broccoli in ways to make it more pleasurable, such as adding spices or sauces?

The profound connection between love and pleasure can be demonstrated scientifically by measuring our physical responses. Our heart rate and respiration actually change when we see loved ones after a separation. A good movie or a good laugh can evoke a similar physiological response. Pleasurable objects and activities stimulate the loving part of ourselves.

The Chemistry of Love

We say there is "spark" to love, and that lovers should have good "chemistry." These are not just metaphors. It may be unromantic to contemplate, but it's important to remember that we are animals, with genetic, physical, and biological needs. I say this because a big part of falling in love is actually chemical.

Our bodies go through specific physiological responses when we are in love. Hormones are released. Our nerve endings become more sensitive. Our heart rate and breathing increase. Our senses actually become heightened. We even smell different.

Since a major part of the experience of love involves these physical sensations, we can begin to create love in ourselves by doing what we can to re-create these responses in our bodies.

This may sound like cheating, but it's not. In fact, it is difficult, if not impossible, to attract love into your life if you are not already in love. By stimulating those parts at the beginning, by experiencing pleasure, you will create in yourself a physical state that will attract others.

So you see, in your love life, you can have your cake and eat it too.

Become a Love Magnet!

Since pleasure is the first step to falling in love, even something as self-indulgent as receiving a massage will help get you started. Seeking pleasure does not mean becoming hedonistic. The point is that once you are in love with yourself, you become open to attracting other people—you actually become more attractive.

Creating pleasure is desirable not only as an end in itself, but also because it creates in us a state that attracts love! On a strictly biochemical level, your body will be secreting the same kinds of chemicals and hormones (fancy neurotransmitters with hard-to-pronounce names like serotonin, oxytocin, and endorphins) that you would if you were in love.

People in love are the ones who attract love. Think about it. If you walk out of the house angry or suspicious, the chances of your attracting a compatible, available, giving lover are slim. People who are able to feel pleasure are the ones who attract pleasure. Pleasure creates in us a chemical state at a profound level that signals to ourselves and others that we are attractive. We seek love in order to receive pleasure. In a evolutionary sense, pleasure was the signal that told us that we were "on the right track." Our bodies literally send out signals that we are ready to both give and receive pleasure, and those around us respond in kind.

Focusing on Pleasurable Interactions

No matter what situation you find yourself in, you can choose to focus on its pleasurable aspects while still being aware of the whole. I dislike washing dishes (one of the world's great understatements), so when I find myself doing them I focus on the smell of the soap and the warmth of the water instead of the odious task at hand.

Once you consciously set about to scan your environment and activities for pleasure, you will find it soon becomes a habit that— surprise—actually increases the amount of pleasure you experience in your life. You may also find that you rework the way you approach your experiences, looking for more subtle ways to enhance the pleasure you find.

Actively looking for pleasure—and expecting to find it—may seem hard to do at first. I discovered how powerful this technique is during an especially difficult time in my life when I was doing many things that I didn't want to do, some of which were downright painful. I didn't have enough time to do any of the things that had given me pleasure in the past, and when I did have a little extra time I was so sleep-deprived that I chose rest over almost anything else. I did not want to become a machine, so I began to look for what I could enjoy in the most mundane or even dreadful situation. Sometimes the only thing I could take solace in was my endurance in the face of hardship.

During those times of unalloyed pleasure, such as playing with my son or sleeping, I made a concerted effort to be totally available to the experience and did not allow these times to be interrupted. I also tried to find little ways to magnify the pleasure I was able to extract, such as at bedtime scenting my pillows and getting a buttery soft pair of pajamas, or making a point of finding an activity my son and I could mutually enjoy such as reading, cooking, making art from found objects, or building a city from Lego blocks.

You May Have to Give Yourself Permission to Find Pleasure

Most of life is mundane unless you consciously allow it to be enjoyable. There is pleasure to be found in virtually every experience, though it may take some searching to discover. If the experience is receiving a painful flu shot, for example, we must focus on the payoff: a relatively healthy winter. Sometimes we must focus on another person's pleasure, or on achieving something that is difficult.

But the pleasure is always there to be experienced, though it is not limited to any one description. The question for your intuition, as well as for your conscious and unconscious minds, should always be, How can I experience pleasure at this moment?

I know this isn't as easy as it sounds. As we learned in doing the first exercise, creating pleasure in our lives often raises many deep-rooted issues. It is especially difficult to create pleasure when we feel the emptiness and pain of not having a lover. We often torture ourselves when we want to be in love. Sometimes we blame ourselves. We feel unworthy or undeserving. Ironically, we create a mental and emotional state—which, in turn, creates a physical state—both of which work against our attracting others and finding love.

Sometimes we need to confront obstacles to pleasure, such as depression or anxiety. If you find yourself truly unable to find pleasure in anything, you may need to seek help for depression. In the meantime, experiment with anything you can think of—massage, aromatherapy, biofeedback, a cup of coffee with a good friend, even a good cry—to reconnect with pleasure.

Developing a Pleasure Habit

You can learn to find pleasure in everyday experiences, even if it seems that you have nothing in your life at all. Even if your life is miserable, you're already in love with something: something in your life fascinates and attracts you.

That's your starting point for love. Maybe what fascinates you and draws you in is simply looking at other people in love and wishing you were, too. You have something that is stimulating you. Step One is to find that something.

Our society continually associates love with denial. We're not good enough. We're not rich enough. If you're overweight and food gives you pleasure, I wouldn't just eliminate certain foods entirely, as we typically do. Instead, I would tell you to get the food you love the most and take a tiny taste every half hour or as needed. You'd consume fewer calories and get more pleasure.

Difficult times are good teachers. Although it may sound surprising, during the most difficult and lonely few years of my life, I learned the most about pleasure:

- I learned to take pride in my strength during crisis. I noticed skills and parts of me that I had never needed to use and therefore had never seen, and I allowed myself to take pride in them.

- I learned to let go of what was not functional in my life. This left me spending time and energy only on what was truly significant.

- I learned about the pleasure of catnaps. I also learned how to work and relax at the same time: doing a phone interview while lying in bed, writing in a pastry shop, doing business on my cell phone while watching my son play in the park with his "pals."

- I learned to use moments of grief effectively—allowing myself tears, learning to accept the comfort of others, and knowing to appreciate these moments of caring as fully as I could.

- Whenever I would think about the injustices in my life, I learned also to recognize my good fortune.

- I learned to taste my food more, and to buy soap that was comforting (I love coconut oil).

And during this hard time, I met a man with whom I was able to share both love and pleasure more fully than I ever had before.

Pain is not a prerequisite for pleasure, but without it you need to be consciously looking for what soothes and delights you. In times of difficulty, pleasure becomes necessary for our well-being, and can even be a survival tool. So we aggressively find pleasure sources, sometimes unconsciously, that we might have otherwise overlooked or experienced only superficially.

It's important not to wait until difficult times to seek pleasure, thereby making pleasure merely a means of relieving pain.

Reconnecting with Forgotten Pleasures

Today our lives are so rushed and busy that we've gotten out of touch with what truly gives us pleasure. I'm not talking about the fleeting satisfactions of acquiring something new or a job well done, but rather those thoughts, perceptions, and experiences that allow us to feel being alive on a gut, visceral level.

You can't fool your pleasure centers. If you're wearing high heels because you want to look a certain way, but your deeper value is comfort, the most lovely pair of high heels won't give you pleasure. Going to the theater gives one person pleasure but is a total bore for another.

The next exercise will reintroduce you to the experience of pleasure, the most important part of falling in love.

EXERCISE 2: GETTING IN TOUCH WITH HOW YOU
EXPERIENCE PLEASURE

Start this exercise by finding a pleasant place to sit or lie down. Remove any possible interruptions to your upcoming experience of pleasure. Unplug your phone, put on snuggly pajamas, light a candle—whatever does it for you. You can use a notebook or a tape recorder for this exercise.

Take a long deep breath and let it out slowly. Notice your nose and then your sense of smell. What are you smelling in your environment right now? As you inhale, notice which scents are pleasurable and which are not.

As you continue to breathe, allow your intuition to give you a scent, a smell that is exquisitely pleasurable for you. Stop for a moment to record what that is.

Now, allow yourself to notice the inside of your mouth. Your tongue, the back of your teeth, your palate. Allow yourself to become aware of all the taste buds in your mouth and what they are tasting at this moment. As you do this, allow your intuition to give you a taste of the most pleasurable taste you can imagine.

As you breathe, allow your eyes to notice what is in the room. What are you looking at? What gives you pleasure to see? What disturbs you? What colors, forms, shapes, movements, do you enjoy?

Now allow yourself to notice what is the most pleasurable thing your senses can take in. As you continue, allow yourself to notice your ears right down to your ear canal. Notice how your ears extend their perceptions through your entire body. Notice what you are hearing in your environment: both what's pleasurable and what's disturbing. Now allow your intuition to give you the sound that's the most pleasurable to you.

Now begin to notice your body. Notice the position you're in and how it feels. Allow yourself to shift positions. Notice the feeling of your skin, your nails, the hair on your head. Notice your eyelashes and the feeling of blinking.

Notice which sensations in your body are the most pleasurable to you. Notice the sensations in your body that are bringing you pleasure in this moment and the ones that are not. Notice which positions, which feelings, give you the most pleasure, and record these.

Now allow your attention to drift to the times in your life when you have experienced the most pleasure. As you do so, consider the following questions:

- *Where were you?*
- *What time of year was it? Were you indoors or outdoors?*

- *What were you doing?*
- *Were you with anyone? Whom?*
- *How did you feel about yourself at this time? About the world?*
- *What were you experiencing with your five senses?*

Asking yourself questions like this will reveal patterns to your needs for pleasure.

Now I'd like you to notice which memories you find most pleasurable, and record at least two or three. Search for memories that evoke pleasure in all your senses. Are these the memories that come to mind most during the day?

I'd like you to notice the thoughts you are having now. Allow your intuition to supply the thoughts that are the most pleasurable for you. How often do you indulge these memories?

Take your time with this exercise. Allow your intuition to continue to provide any other information as you simply notice and record your impressions.

One Person's Example

Here's a partial list of things that evoke feelings of love and pleasure for me: fragrant flowers; the taste of honey; comedy clubs; sitting around with my friends chatting; eating pastries in the park; massages; dancing alone; getting surprises in the mail; making care packages for friends; seeing my family all together; reminiscing with my childhood friends.

Discussion

This exercise will illuminate some of the things and memories and activities that give you pleasure. You may be surprised to rediscover long-forgotten activities that gave you pleasure. I know I was! I remembered being a young child and loving to wake up to the early morning sun coming in through the window by my bed. I then realized how that one repeated experience had heightened many of my memories. I immediately moved my bed from the center of the room to the window.

When you know what gives you pleasure you can do more of it, slipping it into your everyday experiences. For example, a reflexologist friend of mine showed me how to give myself a two-minute relaxing hand massage on the train! Revisit this list frequently. There are infinite possibilities for pleasure. Trade your list with a friend so that you can provide each other with pleasurable experiences.

Remember to Smile and Laugh

While we're on the subject of re-creating the physiological state of love, another way we can achieve this state is by laughing. Why do both men and women value a sense of humor so highly? Why is a great smile sexy? Why is everyone inexplicably drawn to someone laughing?

The next time you're at a party or another social gathering, I'll bet you're attracted to the person laughing and having fun. Even in a more casual setting like a restaurant, we tend to notice most the people having a good time. The old saying is true: laugh and the world laughs with you; cry, and you cry alone.

Joy is inherently attractive; we are almost compelled to gravitate toward it. Why? The biochemical principles are identical. When we laugh our body produces the same kind of chemicals as when we have a massage, dance, or do other pleasure-producing activities. You look different. You smell different. You're producing different chemicals.

Smiles and laughter are powerful aphrodisiacs. Just as you're attracted to others when they're experiencing pleasure, if you experience pleasure, others will be attracted to you. Even a simple smile creates profound changes in your biochemistry. Feeling good makes us smile, and scientists know that the simple act of smiling in turn makes us feel good. It works both ways.

The physical act of laughing actually releases chemicals in our body associated with joy. Think about what or who last made you laugh. What kind of books or experiences make you laugh? If you look for laughter you will find it, and you will put your unconscious on notice to highlight the joy in life

---

EXERCISE 3: LAUGH AND THE WORLD LAUGHS WITH YOU

For the next few days, make a point of noticing other people laughing. Notice how people around them respond. Notice your own responses. You may want to record your observations and experiences in your journal.

Now that you've had practice observing others laughing, do so yourself. Take your funniest book to work and read it on the way or during lunch. Observe how others respond to you. Notice whom you attract.

One Person's Example

At first, paying attention to the laughter of others simply made me more aware of my own deep sadness. Then I remembered the exercise. I noticed that the person laughing had the attention and interest of those around them. Many times someone would try to find out why the person was laughing. I noticed people smiling at the person who was laughing.

I went on a hunt for a funny book, but nothing made me laugh until I found a tape of a popular comedian and popped it in my Walkman for my morning exercise walk. I'm sure that many of the passersby who saw me giggle uncontrollably thought I should be institutionalized. But others responded to me in ways I had not experienced in ages: laughing at me (kindly), laughing with me, starting conversations. I realized how much the quiet expression of my own misery had isolated me. Here I am, expressing the same energy through laughter—but now people are responding positively.

Exercising Regularly Will Make You Literally More Attractive

I'm not talking here about the obvious benefit of exercise making you look better. Scientists now know that regular exercise not only produces many of the same chemicals we mentioned earlier, such as endorphins, our natural painkillers, but it also stimulates the immune system. (Incidentally, by some unknown mechanism, laughter also stimulates the immune system.)

Scientists also know, and we'll discuss this more in the next chapter, that we are genetically programmed to seek out others with strong immune systems. Mother Nature realized a long time ago that if a species is going to survive, it's important that genes get passed on to the healthiest members. From a biological standpoint, it's more important to our species for women to be healthy than for men, since women bear the children. This may explain why men seem to value physical appearance more than women do—because physical appearance is a reliable indicator of physical and genetic health.

So start exercising regularly. Don't go overboard and beat yourself up at the gym. The exercise should be enjoyable and satisfying. You'll feel better, you'll look better, and you'll be healthier to boot.

Don't Forget the Pleasures of Friendship

We also need to feel friendship and connection. It's quite possible that the cause of men having a shorter life span is not just hormonal but rather stems from the fact that men do not connect with others as much as they need to. Women, on the other hand, seem to be more aware that connection is important and life giving. We all need to increase our sense of connection, not only with other people, but also with our environment and with ourselves. Enduring relationships are really about sustaining that connection.

That's important. This book is not just for someone who wants the perfect marriage. If I had to pick one problem in relationships today, it would be that our mates are often the last people we imagine being friends with. This is all the more ironic, since we live in a time when men and women, women and women, and men and men can now all connect and communicate on more intimate levels than was acceptable in previous generations.

Remember to Smell the Roses

As you continue on your pleasure-creating odyssey, I want you to allow yourself to become more aware of your senses. Heightening your sensory awareness will intensify and elaborate your pleasure, since we experience pleasure largely, though not exclusively, through our senses. As we've already discussed, love takes place on a biochemical level. Men as well as women are genetically programmed to literally sniff out desirable mates. Did you know that a woman's senses are more acute when she is ovulating? It's true. And the most expensive cologne or perfume cannot change the genetic markers in the subtle odors our bodies produce.

Knowing what you smell and see and taste and feel is an important first step in being able to make contact with your environment, and in being able to know when that contact is positive. We've even lost contact with our own bodies. Knowing how much and what kind of contact is acceptable and pleasurable to those around you can help you interact more powerfully and joyfully with all that is in your life, while providing and receiving the nourishment that contact offers in the process.

A good friend of mine, for example, gets enormous pleasure from playing chess and the intellectual contact he gets from the other players. Another friend would be tortured at having to stay still for an hour-long massage but never passes up a ten-minute shoulder rub. Maybe your pleasure comes from social dancing or from immersing yourself in a good book.

As much as possible, every aspect of your life should feed your senses. Listen to live music or to the voices of friends. Go on a nature walk. Admire beauty. Make an effort to connect visually with your environment. Fill your home with scents you enjoy or find a perfume or aftershave that delights your senses. Notice the scent of the people you love. Hold hands with a friend. Enjoy the taste of your mouth as you eat food you love. Increase the contact and the pleasure with your environment, yourself, and your senses.

You can nourish your senses simply by becoming aware of them. What do you like to taste, feel, hear, smell, and see? Which kind of sensory stimulation gives you the most pleasure? Soft violet colors give me a sense of well-being, and certain audiotapes that I listen to remind me of that feeling in other moments. I collect flowers in the summer and I dry them and hang them by my bed, and the scent is with me the whole year. I take one of my pillowcases with me wherever I go because I like the feel and scent of my own bed when I am staying in a hotel.

Incidentally, a wonderful way to deepen a relationship is to get to know which kinds of sensory stimulation your partner enjoys. You may discover some differences. I love sweet incense, but it suffocates my partner. He likes citrus scents, which always remind me of clean bathrooms. On the other hand, we both like soft, silky fabrics.

Your Most Important Sense: Touch

It is through touch that we have the strongest connection to others and to our environment. It is the first sense that develops, and in old age it is often the last sense we lose. Through touch we not only communicate but also receive nourishment. Touch is so important to life that infants who receive minimal physical contact fail to thrive and sometimes die. Unfortunately, we live in a society where people are actually taught to avoid this life-sustaining contact.

Of course, some of this is cultural. A recent study in which people were observed to determine the number of times they made physical contact with their companion—whether the companion was their child, lover, or friend—found that Americans touch significantly less than most of our European counterparts. I've experienced this firsthand.

I spent many years in Italy, where men embrace upon meeting and women hold hands on the street. At first I was surprised, but after a while I decided to try it out myself. Initially I was very self-conscious, but now it has become a comfortable part of my behavior.

Touch may not mean that you throw your arms around every friend that you see. We all connect with our environment in our own way and at our own comfort level. It is also important to respect the physical boundaries of others. It may mean putting your hand briefly on the arm of a friend during conversation. Only you know the kinds of touch that are most nourishing and least threatening to you. One woman took ballroom dance classes, another exchanged foot massages with friends.

Opportunities for positive physical touch are around us all the time. Sadly, I've recently become aware that people are losing the habit of shaking hands when they meet. Perhaps it's a sign of the general decline of social manners, but it seems a shame that even that opportunity for a small amount of contact is becoming obsolete.

DAILY REMINDER

Make the decision to seek pleasure every day. You can do this in small ways, in everyday activities. It's important that you learn to find pleasure everywhere. In short, make seeking pleasure a habit. *Smile. Laugh. Exercise. And become aware of your senses, especially your sense of touch.*

Introducing the Millennium Dating Service

The Millennium Dating Service has had windfall business since opening its doors in the year 2000. You sit in the wine-colored velvet sofa and await your turn. The scent of orange blossoms, jasmine, and cinnamon diffuses through the air from an atomizer in the center of the room. Your eyes feel heavy. As you take a deep breath and gently close them, you detect a slow, faint pulse to the music from the speaker in the floor, a pulse that you feel mirrored in your entire body.

What a contrast from your first interview. When you registered, your blood was taken and your face photographed from all angles. The extensive questionnaire you had to fill out seemed more like a psychiatric form than a dating service survey. Who cares what qualities you loved in your mother and father, or how many siblings you have? Who remembers family illnesses three generations back? Then there was that thing that looked like a gas mask that they put on you. They asked you to describe scents in detail and to give your reaction to each. You were surprised that they smelled, well, human.

As you sink more deeply into the couch the scent surrounds you, which seems strange after weeks of following the instructions to use only scent-free detergents, shampoos, and soaps and to wear no perfume or perfumed products. You had to go off the pill, too, and report your menstrual cycle each month. Now the time has arrived.

A woman dressed in blue appears and escorts you to a small changing area. You're given a white toga and told to change. You're then led to a spare dining area with about forty other people, men and women, all dressed in togas like yours. The absence of color, sound, and scent is striking in contrast to the lush room where you've just spent the last few hours.

All your senses are heightened. You know that you will spend the next forty-eight hours with the people who are now seated with you at the table. You select these activities from the schedule in front of you. A comedian will perform after lunch, and then there will be "Roman Games" for the men with the women as spectators. No showers are allowed for the next few days, and just about everything you have been given is unscented. Your mint-flavored toothpaste was confiscated at the door as if it were a contraband drug.

The Millennium Dating Service is an imaginary creation, of course, but it illustrates the profound biological nature of love. Although imaginary, it is entirely plausible.

The Four Types of Attraction

As you begin to get in touch with how you experience pleasure, you should start noticing whom you find attractive and under what circumstances.

We are attracted to—and often find ourselves in love with—people who reinforce our preexisting self-image. If I see myself as a generous person, I will be attracted to people who reinforce that perception. Unfortunately, if I see myself as unworthy of love, I'll find myself attracted to individuals who reinforce that self-image. In more positive terms, we are attracted to people who see us the way we want to be seen, or the way we'd like to be able to see ourselves. These idealized self-images, of course, are often the antithesis of what we *believe* ourselves to be.

Attraction takes place on four levels: physical, physiological, psychological, and spiritual. In any given situation, of course, there may be more of one of these qualities than of another. But none of the qualities of attraction can function independently of the others. For example, psychology can feed physiology, which can shut down spirituality, only to be pushed ahead by the physical. Each of us is a system. All of our parts work together. This is why it's essential to engage all of these parts in any voyage into the discovery of love.

Physical Attraction

The most obvious kind of attraction, the one most celebrated in romance novels, is of course purely physical. We are attracted to someone's smile, or hands, or their legs. Over time, we discover that we "simply prefer" dark hair, or strong legs, or green eyes, or whatever.

Although some of these are undoubtedly personal aesthetic preferences, they are to a great degree intermingled with other physiological or even psychological factors. For example, a woman may be attracted to green eyes because her father's eyes were green. Since the purely physical characteristics that we find attractive are usually pretty obvious, I would like to spend more time discussing the subtler, even unconscious factors.

Physiological Attraction

Without getting too technical, a great deal of sophisticated scientific research has revealed that we tend to be attracted to genetically dissimilar mates. Hence the truth behind the old adage that "opposites attract." This genetic mixing makes good sense from an evolutionary standpoint, where the meeting of similar yet defective genes could spell disaster for the survival of our species.

We are not consciously aware of this genetic screening. After all, it's not as if someone's genetic makeup is stamped on his or her fore-head. In fact, the sense that tells us someone has passed the genetic litmus test is our olfactory sense: the nose. This ability is heightened to a great degree when we are ready to be pregnant, which again makes sense from an evolutionary standpoint. I've often wondered if the best time for men and women to date would be during ovula-tion—the man would get the chemical signal that the woman was fertile, and the woman would be especially attuned to promising genetic partners. (Although she might be in somewhat of a hurry to fertilize that egg!)

So if you're thinking seriously about someone you've just met, schedule a date around this time. (Here's another fact you should know: the birth control pill can short-circuit this genetic matching process to such a degree that a woman on the pill could, hypotheti-cally, be attracted to a man and marry him—only to discover when she later goes off the pill that she suddenly finds him "unattractive.")

Scientists have also discovered that there are other genetically based factors that influence attraction on a subconscious level, many of which have been "encoded" in values of beauty that cross all cul-tural boundaries. For example, the important factor in attracting men is not the absolute size of a woman's waist or her hips, but the ratio of these two measurements. Apparently this relationship is an indica-tor of a woman's overall health, a critical factor from an evolutionary point of view.

I'm not saying, of course, that your primary concern when choos-ing a love partner should be how well you two contribute to the survival of the human species. But keep in mind that sometimes the reason you are attracted to someone has nothing to do with his or her sense of humor or eye color. As biologists say, we are "hardwired" as animals to find certain individuals attractive.

Psychological Attraction

We tend to pick mates who match our level of emotional maturity. Each person selects a mate from a unique psychological agenda. Sometimes we are attracted to people who allow us the opportunity to resolve unfinished business from our first intimate relationships, those with our parents and siblings.

Some of us look for partners who enhance our own false but dearly held beliefs or wishes about ourselves. The typical example of this is the couple in which one partner is significantly older than the other. The older partner often chooses the younger one to convince himself that he's not getting older and nearer to death. The younger partner chooses the older one because he seems willing and able to do for her what she feels she can't do for herself. Of course, this particular dynamic is not limited to couples with large age differences.

Numerous unconscious psychological scenarios influence our attractions. The more psychologically (and chronologically) "mature" we are, the more likely we are to pick a mate who embodies what we find of value in the world. Until we reach that maturity, we are not predetermined to play out our unconscious agendas. By bringing into our conscious mind what we're looking for in a mate, and then allowing ourselves to work with that "picture"—emotionally, psychologically, and intuitively—we take the first step to being guided by our conscious rather than our unconscious needs. As you do the exercises in this book, you'll notice your unconscious scenarios being replaced by a more psychologically sound and emotionally nourishing attraction scenario.

Spiritual Attraction

From time to time, it's important to take stock of our beliefs and values:

- What do I consider important?
- Why am I doing what I'm doing?
- What is my destiny?

How you view your destiny may change many times over the course of your life, but the essential values that characterize your destiny will not change much as your life progresses. When you think about relationships in conjunction with your destiny, you are looking deep down for someone who understands your path and can walk it beside you. This does not mean that your mate has to be on exactly the same path as you, but simply on a path that makes room for your values. I believe that many disastrous relationships occur because people are initially attracted to each other on a spiritual level, where they perceive a likeness and compatibility. This initial reaction is not bound by experience or chemistry, and the couple turns out to be psychologically or physiologically incompatible.

The following exercise will help make you more aware of the attraction process.

EXERCISE 4: GETTING BEYOND ANIMAL ATTRACTION

For the next few days or weeks, observe whom you find attractive—and under what circumstances. If you are in a relationship, this may not include your partner. That's fine. Just because you find another individual attractive doesn't mean you must act on that attraction! To the extent that you can, notice whether your attraction is primarily physical, physiological, psychological, or spiritual.

Creating Pleasure in Our Lives Requires a Conscious Commitment

I have so many odds and ends to do all of the time that I have to make a conscious decision to recognize what is pleasurable in my life and what I have to feel good about. Perhaps you do, too. All in all, your fantasy life and your everyday life may not be too far apart. But each day you must deliberately set aside time for yourself and do pleasurable things. You must also notice the things that are in your life in which you could be taking pleasure.

Again, these needn't be extravagant activities. Spending five minutes listening to your favorite music or recollecting one of your favorite memories will be enough to create pleasure—and much of the physiological experience of love. The Italians have a saying: "He who contents himself enjoys." Find ways to take pleasure and contentment in what is available to you, and your journey toward love will become both more effective and more pleasurable.

Your first exercise, then, should be practiced on a daily basis.

⅗ DAILY PRACTICE

Finding Pleasure in Everyday Life
Review your first two exercises. You've reminded yourself of all the things that give you pleasure. Now add these things to your life. You don't have to set aside a fixed block of time from your regular schedule. But do make a conscious commitment to experience pleasure as often as possible, ideally at least once every hour.

Putting It All Together

Of course, there is a lot more to finding true love than simply creating pleasure and becoming more attractive. Still, it's important to remember that you are your most attractive when you're truly enjoying yourself. In our search for love, it is easy to lose sight of the activities and friends we have that give us pleasure. What's more, knowing that we can find pleasure ourselves reminds us of our independence, increasing our self-confidence, which increases our attractiveness even more. And if you're already involved, your ability to find pleasure and enhance your attractiveness will add spice to a satisfying relationship, and perhaps even rekindle a less satisfying one.

Now that you're actively creating love in your life, you're ready to move on to the next step: discovering who you are and what you want in love. Before we do so, however, you'll need a crash course in using intuition.

Checklist

⅗ I create pleasure and the state of love in my life every day.

INTERMISSION

Love Byte

Tuning into Others—and Yourself

Your intuition operates all the time, though you may not be aware of it. It's important to gain conscious control over it. Otherwise it will work toward your unconscious goals, some of which may be undesirable.

In the following two chapters, you'll learn how to use your intuition as an antenna to help you find and enhance love. In addition to receiving *signals from potential compatible partners,* your intuition enables you to send *signals to others,* too. This ability is commonly referred to as telepathy. You'll learn how to send out signals telepathically, letting compatible partners know you're available. And if you're in a relationship, you'll learn how to send signals in a way your partner can respond to. You'll also learn to respond to signals he may not know he is sending.

Like your intuition, your telepathic ability operates all the time. Each moment of the day, you send out signals to your environment and those in it. If you're not enjoying the love you want, it's very possible that you have inadvertently been sending the wrong message to others. In this chapter you'll learn not only how to communicate telepathically, but also what to communicate.

◌❦ 2 ❦◌

A Crash Course in
Using Your Intuition

Intuition and Love

Because intuition provides us with invaluable information that cannot be gained through other means, it can help us immeasurably in finding and enhancing love. For example, it might simply alert us to go to a party after declining the invitation, letting us know that someone we need to meet will be there. But intuition can also help us in more profound ways, including the following:

- Intuition can enable us to make a new acquaintance feel understood and appreciated on first contact.

- Intuition helps us sense immediately which of our qualities to highlight in order to attract a certain person and to find points of common interest.

- Intuition enables us to uncover someone else's needs and passions, and to know how best to satisfy them.

- Intuition helps us to know our own life path. It allows us to sense what kind of mate we will need or want in the future, leading us to potential partners we might have overlooked. Intuition also enables us to know where to find such individuals.

- Finally, intuition helps put us in touch with our own personal issues that may be getting in the way of finding a satisfying relationship. It also provides us with tools we need to address those issues.

In short, to know what you want, and what your ideal partner wants, intuition is an indispensable aid. Your intuition operates all the time, whether you are aware of it or not. And since your intuition can work either for you or against you in love, you'd better get in touch with it.

What Exactly Is Intuition?

There's nothing esoteric about intuition. It's an ability we all have—a means of gaining information about others, ourselves, and our environment that would not otherwise be accessible to us.

Your intuition operates all the time. It does so without your conscious direction by bringing important information to your attention.

How it does so is not entirely clear, but consider the following questions: What if your senses extended farther than you realized? What if you were more connected to things "far away" than you thought? What if everything—everything—you noticed had meaning? If you accept these premises, you can accept the existence of intuition.

One reason intuition is viewed with some distrust is that it's misunderstood and often confused with its characteristics. Just because intuitive impressions usually precede rational thought doesn't mean everything that precedes rational thought is intuition! Saying something "off the top of your head" does not necessarily mean you're being intuitive. It's important that we be systematic in our approach.

The Intuitive Process in a Nutshell

Since our intuition operates all the time, our real goal is to take conscious control of our intuitive process. We will then begin to develop the habit of using our intuitive perception. Yet even people who believe in intuition have difficulty accepting the possibility that it can be controlled. Because they have not yet trained their intuition, they view it as something that strikes randomly, out of the blue, and therefore cannot be relied upon.

The intuitive process is actually quite simple:

Step 1: Do a quick "body check" to get centered. This need not take more than a few seconds to a few minutes at most. All you're doing is tuning in to your current awareness of yourself to give yourself a baseline to judge how your intuitive awareness shifts in response to a specific question. Notice what you are perceiving with your five senses—touch, taste, smell, sight, and hearing—as well as what thoughts, memories, and feelings you are aware of.

Step 2: Focus on a specific question. Frame your question carefully; in other words, know what you are asking. Beware of asking "leading" questions such as "Will I marry Jake in the next two years?" To get an objective reading, it is better to ask, "Whom will I be romantically involved with two years from now?"

Step 3: Notice your first impressions—even "distractions." I have distractions in quotes because any impressions you receive are not distractions but rather important information. Once you present your intuition with a question, everything you think, sense, remember, or perceive in any other way is information to help you find an answer. Allow yourself to notice and record in some fashion, by either writing or taping, everything that you are aware of internally and in your environment. Of course this awareness will shift and change from moment to moment. Your attention will naturally focus on the perceptions/information that is pertinent to your question. Remember: you are pretending that everything is meaningful. Keeping this in mind will broaden your perceptions.

Step 4: Interpret your impressions. Intuition rarely speaks to us in direct statements like "Ask Robert out on a date" or "My partner is feeling neglected"—especially if we're unaccustomed to listening to it. Some people receive their intuition visually, in symbols. Others receive it through their sense of hearing, or perhaps kinesthetically, through their body. Often it is a combination of different senses, thoughts, and memories that provides you with information. Your information may not make sense to you at first. Assemble your information as you would the pieces of a puzzle. Assume that your informaion is correct and your job is to interpret and assemble the pieces until they make sense to you. Learn to get in touch with the unique language and symbols your intuition uses. And since your impressions may not make immediate sense, you'll need to review them and reinterpret them from time to time.

The fourth step takes some practice. Here's an example of how it might work. Let's say you direct your intuition with a question about what will happen in your current relationship, which is going through a difficult time. You notice the front wheels of a car turned in your direction. But as you look further, you see the car is not heading directly at you and puts you in no great danger. You smell the peaches next to you and notice that the timer on your oven has ten minutes left until it signals that your dinner is ready.

As you interpret these impressions, you find that your relationship difficulties are not "aimed at you." Your intuition is signaling that you need to allow things to evolve naturally. You must put your energy into accepting what develops instead of wasting energy trying to figure out what might happen. This intuitive information may in turn help you see other signals—empirical or emotional—in your relationship. These signals may have been overlooked because you had personalized the difficulty. We, as human beings, are "hardwired" to find the information we need. Your intuition will use anything it can to cue you to that information.

We'll talk about the importance of verifying your intuition and integrating it into your decision-making process shortly.

Keeping Your Processes Distinct: Intuition First, Then Logic, Then Emotions

One reason we don't consciously use our intuition more often is that we usually have so much information to work with. For beginners to notice their intuition, it's best not to have any kind of information about your target.

To give accurate readings, with a minimum of judgments or emotional interference, and to keep your thinking clear, you must strive for a detached perspective. To quiet your logical mind, try the following:

- Do "blind intuitive readings" in which you write different questions on slips of paper and place them in numbered envelopes, choosing them at random.
- When you give a reading, speak or take notes continuously so your conscious mind does not have a chance to intervene.

We've become trained over the years to approach things analytically and to ignore our hunches and "unreliable" emotions. This means that the reasoning process can easily overwhelm your intuitive impressions. What's more, our emotions usually crowd out intuition, too.

Your goal then is to train yourself to respond to a question first with intuition, then with logic, then with your emotions. Of course, I don't mean to suggest that intuition is more important or more accurate than either logic or emotion. Rather, the point is simply to keep your emotions and logical mind at bay in order to give your intuition a crack at the problem.

Always Verify Your Intuitive Impressions Before Acting on Them

A common question people ask is "How can I distinguish genuine intuition from, say, a hope or a fear?" Intuition usually comes from a detached perspective. If the impression comes with a strong emotion, it's probably not intuitive even if it comes out of the blue. Also, you'll know your intuition was speaking if it allows you to approach a situation from a perspective different from those offered by analysis or emotion.

You don't have to trust your intuition! Coming from a professional intuitive, this statement always surprises people. The point is that your intuitive impressions can almost always be verified. How? By using intuitive reasoning and then comparing the conclusion to the other data you have available.

Here's how it works: when you receive intuitive information—a hunch, for example—follow it up with questions. Let's say you get a hunch that you should postpone your engagement party because your boyfriend is about to reveal some disturbing news.

Resist the temptation to call the caterer—for now—but don't let your intuition off the hook. Instead, present it with other questions: In what setting will he reveal this disturbing news? What will precede the event? Is this news something that involves "us"? If it does, is it something we can work through? Is my boyfriend already aware of the situation?

By testing and probing your intuition in this way, you give your reasoning mind more information to work with. If these other events don't come to pass, it's likely that your hunch to postpone your engagement was not genuinely intuitive. You can also investigate other, nonintuitive sources of fact such as asking your boyfriend if there is anything on his mind.

Integrate Your Intuitive Information

Once you've completed reporting your impressions you'll need your reasoning ability to make sense of your intuitive impressions and to see how logic can shed light on your question. If your logical conclusions conflict with your gut answers, keep probing with further questions.

You will rarely be in a position where you have to make a decision based solely on intuition. You must learn to balance your intuitive, logical, and emotional processes. Each serves a different function and has different strengths and weaknesses.

Your Intuition Is Goal Directed—for Better or Worse

Intuition is a survival skill. It operates all the time, alerting you to both dangers and opportunities. Your intuition accepts its goals from both your conscious and your unconscious mind without distinction, so it's important that you develop your ability to direct it consciously. If you don't use your intuition in a directed way toward a conscious goal, your unconscious mind will direct it to your hidden agenda. This may be to play out unfinished stories or unresolved conflicts from the past.

For example, one person might be unconsciously using her intuition to keep attracting critical mates as a way of resolving a relationship with her critical mother; another's intuition might be leading her to find withholding mates to punish herself for some unexplored guilt over a past action.

Your unconscious is working through many different objectives at the same time. It's also continually letting your conscious self know what your needs are, even if some of those needs may be outdated. A five-year-old often needs to be reminded about what he can't do or can't have. A forty-year-old does not need to be reminded of those things. But unfortunately his or her unconscious may not know that yet.

The conscious use of intuition repatterns experience and interpretation so that the unconscious learns new, pleasurable, and life-affirming scenarios. Once you give your intuition a task, such as finding a good relationship or improving the one you have, it will be alert to everything that can help you reach that goal.

If You Have Trouble Accepting the Existence of Intuition, Pretend

Some people have difficulty accepting the existence of intuition, but until you are convinced of your intuition's power—and I'm sure you will be if you aren't already—simply keep an open mind. What do you have to lose? If I'm right, you open up your intuition and expand both your sources of information and your means of communication. If I'm wrong, you'll at least become more aware of your surroundings. You'll also have become attuned to the messages you are communicating, consciously and unconsciously, verbally or intuitively.

By the way, if you are not skilled in the conscious use of intuition, don't be discouraged if you aren't reading people's minds next week! You may be frustrated by some of the intuitive exercises at first. Don't worry. With practice your intuitive awareness will expand, and in the meantime these exercises will spark your imagination and offer additional insights into yourself, your needs, and others. A more comprehensive training in intuition can be gained by doing the exercises in my fist book *Practical Intuition.*

An Intuitive Lesson I Learned in My Son's Nursery School

When my son, Samson, started nursery school, there was a little girl in his class who was difficult to calm once she became upset. The teachers were wonderfully solicitous at such times and carried her around, singing and whispering words of comfort and encouragement in her ear. Despite their best efforts, however, she remained inconsolable.

The class was composed of two-year-olds, but she was a little younger than her peers. I wondered if it could be her age that made the teachers' expressions of comfort fall on deaf ears. One day, Samson was having a particularly hard time being left at school. So instead of leaving when I dropped him off, I remained for a while. To be fair, I played with all of the children.

It wasn't long before the little girl began to cry. Samson did not want me to pick her up because I was "his mommy." I thought that maybe singing a song might help. For some reason I chose a song that I had learned in Hebrew school many years before.

The little girl immediately brightened up. The teachers were so amazed by my apparent "magic" with the little girl that they drifted over to listen to my less-than-melodic voice.

"You're incredible with children," one teacher remarked, "none of us has ever been able to calm her down when she gets like that."

I felt like the supreme universal mother. I did, that is, until lunchtime, when her father came to pick her up. I smiled as he knelt down to hug his daughter and began chatting to her—in Hebrew. All of a sudden it was clear: this little girl had not recognized the teacher's English words of comfort and therefore had not been soothed by them. Because she could understand the song in Hebrew, she could accept it as her own.

Intuitive Communication Using I-mode

We've all experienced a kind gesture from another that was not the right sort of kindness to affect us or our feelings. Conversely, we have all felt loved by someone doing the wrong thing but with the right feeling.

It is not just what you say that is important—but what you think and the energy with which you hold yourself and the other person in your mind. Often it's important to send a "full body" message, one that engages all your senses, one in which you feel, see, think, smell, and hear what you're sending in a clear and cohesive way.

I refer to this as I-mode. To do this, you fully embody another person. To do this you don't just step into another's shoes but also into this person's body, and try to feel and perceive his thoughts and perceptions as if they were yours. Once you are able to do this—and you'll have plenty of practice in this book—you will not only have a sense of what he is feeling and thinking, you will also know how best to present your thoughts and feelings to him in a way that will be understood and accepted.

We'll return to intuition briefly in a later chapter. Now let's turn our attention to how we can send messages to others telepathically, and which messages we should send.

Our Second Experiment

Stop!
Complete This Exercise Before Reading Any Further!

EXERCIES 5: CALL ME

Think of someone from whom you would like to receive a phone call. The objective of this exercise is to have your "target" call you within a specified time frame (I recommend a day).

You can use anybody for this exercise—a long-lost friend, your college roommate sophomore year. The only requirement is that the person should not *be someone you're expecting to hear from during the experiment. Of course, it should be someone who has your phone number and who* might *call you.*

I won't give you any clues on how to approach this exercise. Have fun with it. We'll be discussing it in the next chapter.

◈3 ◈

Using Telepathy in Love

Introducing Relationship Telepathy

Until now we've been discussing intuition as an information-gathering ability. Another aspect of your intuitive abilities is telepathy. Telepathy is the ability to transmit thoughts and feelings to another person—even across great distances—and to receive thoughts and feelings in return. It is the most commonly reported and commonly accepted of intuitive experiences. In fact, most people can recall a moment of telepathy in their lives. As with our other intuitive abilities, telepathy occurs most often without our knowledge, though it occurs continually.

The existence of telepathy has been confirmed in scientific studies. In one experiment, scientists were shocked to discover that untrained individuals could actually tell when someone was staring at the back of their heads! In another popular study called remote viewing, which has been replicated numerous times—the CIA spent millions trying to develop it into a spy tool—a remote "receiver" is able to describe in detail a picture or a scene viewed hundreds or even thousands of miles away by a "viewer."

Telepathy is more active than other forms of intuition. Not only are you *receiving* information intuitively, you're *sending* it, too—again, whether you realize it or not. Even alone in your house or apartment, you continually transmit thoughts and feelings that affect the world around you.

Reviewing Our Second Experiment

Everyone has the experience of wanting a romantic interest to call. You wait by the phone; you feel a need for the other person, and you internally demand of him or her, "Call me."

You become increasingly aware of your own desperation. Questions race through your head. "Why isn't he calling?" You begin to feel abandoned, so you try to think of all the reasons why he isn't calling. You can't imagine any. It begins to hurt. "I wish he knew how much I want him to call me," you think. You get more and more upset, and before long you may even become angry. You tell yourself, "If he knew how I felt, he'd call."

But would he? Try the following thought experiment. Pretend for a moment that the other person could actually hear what you're thinking, could actually feel what you're feeling. Would that person really want to get in touch with you? It may actually be the case that the person you're thinking about is perceiving what you are at that moment: an angry, frightened, demanding person pulling at him. If that person were in front of you, would you want to be there? I doubt it.

You can switch roles for a different perspective. Feel someone who desperately needs you. This person is pulling you toward him, perhaps even trying to devour you. How do you respond to this person and the urgency of his desire? Do you want to move closer, or farther away?

Now, instead of waiting by the phone desperately, what if you used your perceptions instead to imagine your romantic interest and feel the connection you share with him? What if you deeply felt the pleasure you both would take in hearing each other's voice and speaking to each other? Remember: relationships must be win-win.

Feel your attitude change—which may be subtle—as you imagine this scenario. He can feel it, too. There may be compelling reasons why he isn't calling, but he's far more likely to respond to a positive message than to a message of desperation.

Again, relationship telepathy isn't mind control. You can't will another person to call you. And desperately wanting him to call will, if anything, give him a reason not to.

Telepathy works best if you use all your senses to send the message: the feeling of needing to call home, seeing the telephone, hearing the phone's ringing, fully embodying the other person with I-mode, and so on. Remember: you're sending telepathic messages all of the time. This exercise involves doing so consciously, and noting your results so that love telepathy can become a reliable tool.

EXERCISE 6: CALL ME, REVISITED

As you did in the first Call Me exercise, think of someone from whom you would like to receive a call. This time use what you have learned about intuition and telepathy.

Begin with a body check. Allow your intuition to reveal to you the feelings or messages that, sent telepathically, would motivate that person to call. Record your information.

Use all of your senses to perceive where the other person is in relation to you. You may "feel" him at the office, or "see" him at home, or "hear" him at a movie. When you can sense where this person is, hold on to that sense as you do another body check.

Now, using all of your senses, allow yourself first to embody the other person and then to send to him the thoughts, feelings, senses, and images that you received in the first part of this exercise. Don't send a perception that could cause the other person discomfort (for example, an emergency might get someone to call, but it wouldn't be a right thing to do unless there's a real emergency).

One Person's Example

The first thing I hear after my body check is the patter of the rain on the window. I feel a heaviness in my heart, a mix of sadness and fear. Still, my head feels happy and optimistic. I smell toast and other early-morning smells. I taste the cinnamon in my coffee. My attention goes to the ring on the third finger of my right hand. My sister gave me the ring, but as a result of an awful argument, we are no longer speaking. I still have fond memories of our childhood together, when we often got up to make breakfast together before our parents arose.

I choose my sister for the telepathic exercise. I get the sense that the feeling of mother, home, comfort, safety, would motivate her to call. I imagine us sitting in the park and sharing a sandwich and talking, and her feeling the connection between us that transcends the problems we have with each other.

I see my sister in a wheat-colored chair in her apartment. Her arm looks bloated. She is silent. She is staring at the stereo in front of her. She needs to get out of the chair, but she doesn't want to.

I embody the feeling of her being safe and secure with me. I saw myself next to her in the chair, her head resting on my shoulder. At first she was tense, but she relaxed when she felt the total acceptance I was offering.

I picture her picking up the phone.

Her Results

Just as I pictured my sister calling me, I was shocked to hear the phone ring. Practically trembling, I picked up the receiver just to find out that it was the local florist wanting to know if he could make a delivery. I did not receive a call from my sister within twenty-four hours. I didn't feel that I could call her because of the rift between us. I repeated this exercise with a good friend. This time it worked immediately, but I had very much hoped that it would work with my sister.

Three weeks later, my sister's husband called—at her behest—to tell me that my sister had been ill and wanted to know if we could speak to each other civilly, without "getting into things." I agreed.

I called her. A few minutes into the conversation, she told me that she had been having a very difficult time and she was remembering how well I had comforted her as a child and had felt a longing for me. After two years of estrangement, we agreed to meet. When we saw each other, it felt as if not a moment had passed and there was no longer any distance between us.

I'm still not sure whether it was her unconscious telepathic message of need that made me choose her for this exercise, or whether it was my telepathic message that allowed her to get in touch with her need. It doesn't matter. Either way, we've started communicating and have reestablished our lifelong bond.

Discussion

You can repeat this exercise often. You needn't wait until you actually want someone to call you. Of course, telepathy can be used in many other ways, but this exercise dramatically demonstrates how telepathy can affect a relationship in subtle and not-so-subtle ways. Our goal is to signal to the environment that we are available for love, and to create a beacon so that those looking for the love signal can find us.

Don't be discouraged if your first attempts don't seem to work. If you didn't receive a call from that person within a day, call him yourself. See whether he tells you, "I was thinking of calling you!" Remember that you cannot telepathically get someone to do something against his or her will, and there may be compelling reasons why the person didn't call that have nothing to do with you. Practice on people who would want to call you anyway. This exercise will bring you results the more you practice, so apply it regularly.

What Kind of Messages Are You Sending?

We unwittingly project our thoughts and feelings far more than we are conscious of—or we'd wish! If you're thinking, "I'm not good enough," or "I'm never going to fall in love," or "That person is prettier," you're transmitting that message to others. If we want telepathy to work for us, we must be especially careful of the thoughts, perceptions, beliefs, and feelings we're putting out there.

You may be thinking that if it was easy to think sunnier thoughts, you would have done it by now. You don't have to obliterate the old patterns of being and thinking completely, but you do need to project other, more positive thoughts and feelings into the messages you *want* to send out. Try to recall, with all of your senses, a memory in which you are happy and joyful. Evoke that memory as frequently as possible.

If you don't have a single memory that represents your ideal state, make a patchwork quilt of memories. You can create a new memory for yourself from these remnants until you have a memory that suits your needs. It's important to use pieces of real memories, instead of simply inventing a fantasy, because real memories include the visceral perceptions of all your senses. You need to remember more than just a picture or a feeling for good telepathy. Experience the smell, sound, touch, feel, taste, look, and rhythm of the memory fully.

The following exercise will help you develop better telepathic communication with others. If you're not currently in a relationship, it will help you send the right telepathic message to prospective mates. When you are clear about who you want your mate to be (which we'll be discussing at length in the next step), ask yourself the following question: "What do I need to embody to attract this person to me?"

Remember to use your own unique attributes to do this. You don't want to attract someone who is going to fall in love with what you're pretending to be. Record the information you receive so that you can refine it and refer to it daily. Then make a practice of embodying the answer.

EXERCISE 7: IT'S NOT JUST WHAT YOU SAY . . .

From time to time, consider the following questions: What messages are you now communicating to others and to your environment? What messages do you want to communicate so that others will respond to you in a way you would like?

You can practice this in your professional as well as your personal life. With a little imagination, you can develop unlimited applications of the telepathy principles you've learned.

Example No. 1

After doing the phone telepathy exercise a few times with good results, I've been using it every day in a variety of situations. For example, I was having difficulty getting my boyfriend to make time for a project we had planned for a long time.

One day, in the middle of a discussion with him, I did a quick body check and asked my intuition what I needed to do to ignite in him a genuine desire to complete our project. I remembered myself in a business meeting the day before in which my manner was clear, direct, and to the point. Additional impressions showed me that this project was charged with so many emotional hang-ups for both of us—his not wanting to be dictated to, my feeling hurt that he wasn't more forthcoming, the stress that the delay had caused both of us—that I had to remove the emotional past from the project and present it in a new light.

I felt myself reexperiencing who I'd been in that business meeting: what my body felt like; the thoughts that I was having; the way I was breathing. I recaptured these sensations and brought them into my body. Later I organized what we'd need to get started. The very next Saturday when we woke up, I let him know that this was a good time to begin our project, much as I'd done at my previous business meeting. We not only started the project that morning, but finished it before the weekend was over.

Example No. 2

I am not currently in a relationship. When I focused my intuition on the personal qualities I needed to attract love, I felt myself peeking out into the sunlight to see what was around me. I realized that in my desperation to find love, I had lost my curiosity about life. It suddenly dawned on me that I needed to ask myself what was interesting about every person, event, and situation in my life, and to focus on my long-lost curiosity.

Sometimes I feel so overwhelmed by the commitments in my life that I cut out what is not essential. I know now that my innate curiosity is not optional; it is the emotion I use to expand my environment. Since practicing this exercise habitually, I have noticed not only that I am more optimistic about life and the people around me but also that people are taking more notice of me.

Example No. 3

I need to embody a readiness to be a partner and have a family. The instability of my childhood made it hard for me to allow people to become irreplaceable. I think my need to avoid becoming too attached prevents me from finding the partner I described in my love goal.

To embody the part of me I need to project, I must go back to a memory of my first truly committed relationship. Although my lover at the time did not respond in the way I had hoped, my primary feeling in the relationship—a single-minded commitment to him and only to him—is the part of me I most need to embody now to attract the right partner.

Discussion

You can ask your intuition different questions for different situations. For example, if you know someone you care about is having a hard time, ask yourself, "What do I need to embody for this person to help her through this crisis?" or, if things feel flat in your relationship, "What do I need to embody to re-create passion with my partner?"

Record both your message and the response. Telepathy does not always work immediately, but keep track of what you send, and you may be happily surprised by the messages you get back.

Be Yourself

We've all known people we would describe as "low key" and others we would describe as "high energy." There is an energy of love, an energy unique to who you are and who you want to attract. Have you ever noticed that when you are in love others fall in love with you? (Where were these people when you were alone?) Your visceral energy of love is attracting these people to you. You create that energy just by thinking of love.

Unfortunately, if your energy is that of wanting love and you are projecting longing and sadness, that is what you attract. I'm not suggesting that you deny your sadness or loneliness, but simply be aware of the message you may inadvertently be sending out.

We've been talking about being in a loving state. Once you're in that state you'll attract love naturally (rather than employing "tricks" or following "rules"). You're allowing yourself to become desirable and sending out a message on all levels that you are available.

It's important to keep in mind that if you're sending a message of something you don't truly believe or feel, you're working outside of the bounds of your integrity—your essential self. In doing so, you're doing both yourself and the other person a disservice.

What's Coming Up

In this chapter, you've begun to learn how to tune into others intuitively, and how to send messages compatible with your love goal to the world. You'll be developing this ability in the coming weeks and months. In future chapters you'll learn different ways you can use both intuition and telepathy in amazingly practical ways. In the meantime, you're now ready to move on to the next step: deciding what you're looking for!

Checklist

- 🕉 I create pleasure and the state of love in my life every day.
- 🕉 I know how to receive intuitive information about myself and others, and how to project telepathically messages compatible with my love goal.

STEP TWO

Creating the Map

Love Byte

Getting Down to Business

If you don't know what you're looking for, the old proverb goes, how will you know when you've found it? Indeed, if you don't know what you're looking for—you may already have it.

People in romantic relationships usually know what's missing. Few, however, know precisely what they want. I've known women who have lived alone for years and then for the first time in their lives fall in love with the man they want. Soon after, however, they're astounded to realize that the joy they feel in their new relationship is strongly tempered by no longer being able to call their closet space their own.

So in this step I'm going to show you how to get in touch with what you really want. Your goal must be more specific than the vague generalities we typically see in personal ads: "I want a tall, handsome, intelligent, successful man, with a great sense of humor." "I want to be married and live in the country and not have to work." "I want a beautiful woman who makes every day exciting."

You'll be imagining your ideal partner and dream relationship. Don't worry, I won't ask you to carve this in stone. Your love goal will change, perhaps greatly, in the coming weeks. But you need a starting point.

If you currently have a partner, be aware that in the process of articulating what you want, you may discover certain aspects missing from your relationship. That doesn't mean your relationship isn't right for you, but it may point to issues you'll both need to address. I'll show you how to do that in Step Five.

Finally, you should be aware that articulating what you want, and envisioning it as a tangible reality, can raise internal issues for you such as fears or insecurities. This is natural, and I will show you how to work through these problems in Step Three.

～4～

Setting Your Love Goal:
Laying the Groundwork

The Two Great Tragedies in Life

According to Oscar Wilde, there are two great tragedies in life: "One is not getting what one wants, and the other is getting it." His warning seems particularly appropriate to our quest.

In my workshops, I am continually amazed at the number of men and women looking for a relationship but who are unable to say what precisely they're looking for beyond some vague, usually clichéd characteristics: "attractive," "funny," "athletic," "supportive." We're not talking about writing a personal ad.

What's more, many people seem not the slightest bit aware of how their unconscious needs express themselves—usually at odds with their conscious goals. Ironically, more often than not people wind up with exactly what they are looking for; the problem is that their conscious selves had one goal while their unconscious selves had another. Whenever it's a contest between these two, the unconscious self usually enjoys a huge edge.

Since the success of your journey begins with your goal, we will be spending this entire step on getting a handle on what you are really looking for in a partner and in a relationship.

Don't Confuse Your Need for Love with Other Needs

The human urge to be in love is primal. Love has the evolutionary value of keeping us and our young safe, and giving us the means of procreation (which, my father kept reminding me half cynically the day I turned thirty, was my "biological destiny"). Four needs that we all share are those of touch, protection, connection, and sensory stimulation (sex of course being a more intense combination of these). Unfortunately, we sometimes confuse our need for one or more of these with our need for romantic love.

The need for human touch is not just a luxury but is a biological necessity. This need is almost as strong as our other physical needs such as the need for food and shelter. Scientists have discovered, for example, that the more a newborn is touched, the healthier it is and the faster it gains weight. Human touch is literally nourishing. We can make a point of increasing our human contact in many ways—giving and receiving massages, longer, warmer handshakes, hugs when greeting those we know, or touching others as we speak with them.

While human contact is undoubtedly the most beneficial form of touch, we can experience touch in other ways through all our senses. For example, we can feel the embrace of nice fabric or a soft lotion on our skin. Or we can be touched by loving sounds and music, by scents and tastes (especially those that evoke pleasant feelings or memories), and by sight, when we have colors around us that we enjoy.

We also need to feel protected. Incidentally, "comfort" and "nourishment" are subtle catchwords for protection, along with the more obvious ones such as money, possessions, strength, and control. A woman might say, "I pretended for a long time that my family really loved me. I used fantasy to feel protected. I found relationships where I was not really valued by my partners, and partners where I was not their priority." On the other hand, a man might say, "I always found women who needed protecting. When they no longer needed protecting, they no longer needed me. Then they would complain that I was smothering them. I felt that I had given a lot, and now it was my turn. I'm learning that I trust money and status, but I don't trust love—so I don't find it."

As you gain greater awareness of what experience you want in a romantic relationship, and as you expand more fully your knowledge of yourself through your growing intuitive awareness, you will find clarity about what you want and need in a partner. The shortest distance between two points *is* a straight line. As you gain a clearer sense of your needs, you will find a more direct path to your partner.

Don't Expect Your Love Life to Satisfy All Your Needs

A major cause of disappointments in relationships is the unconscious if not conscious belief that our love life will fulfill all our needs. Not only is this an unrealistic fantasy, but we must also remember that our love life is merely one part of our life—admittedly a major one.

This fact is often overlooked by people in their hunger for love. What you want in your love life will affect and be affected by what you want in other areas of your life such as your professional life, your friendships and other important relationships, and even your needs as a solitary individual.

In a word, I am talking about the need for balance.

How a Relationship Lets Us Feel about Ourselves

As you begin to think about what you want in a partner, ask yourself how that person makes you feel about yourself. A relationship and being in love allow us to feel and use parts of ourselves that we normally don't get to experience. A relationship is about how we would like to experience ourselves. If you have artistic talent, you will not feel fulfilled unless you can draw on that part of yourself. Similarly, only in a romantic relationship can you experience certain parts of yourself.

So when we say we want to be in love, a big part of that is that we want to be a certain way that is only possible within a love relationship. To a great degree, we want a partner who complements and brings out the best in us.

The next exercise is designed to address this point.

EXERCISE 8: WHAT'S MISSING?

Describe your life right now. Describe how you'd like it to be. Make a list of all the things you feel that are missing in your life right now.

Who are you now and who do you want to be? Make a list of the parts of yourself that you've not been able to experience in your previous (or current) relationships.

I have intentionally made these questions broad to force you to consider your love life in the larger context of your entire life.

One Person's Example

I am a successful business executive. I have a good social life and good friends. I date, but I haven't been able to find someone who I know is, without a doubt, the person I want to spend my life with.

I spend most of my time at work and my free time at the gym. My social life centers around the people I know from work, many of whom are married. I have what I need in many respects: money, friends, looks, health, a good job. Yet my life still doesn't feel like it fits together most of the time.

I would like to be in a relationship. I want mutual passion with my mate. I want us to desire each other when we are together, and miss each other when we are apart.

I would like to buy a home and raise a family. I want a family life. I would like my family to support my career and my career to support my family. I would like to be part of the kind of family I grew up in. We shared our experiences with one another and laughed all the time. We felt respect for one another, and we were interested and invested in one another's accomplishments.

I know I am coming into my own, but I don't quite feel secure with who I am. I sometimes miss the person that I was. I feel ready to share my life with the right person, but I am afraid that I will make bad choices, as I have in the past. I am very responsible. I sometimes feel trapped by all of my self-imposed responsibilities, not to mention the ones that others impose upon me. I am not a risk taker but I am realizing that I sometimes miss out because I avoid change and inevitably also miss opportunities.

I want to feel secure and excited at the same time. I want to know the value of what I have while still being able to challenge the things I value and make changes in them. This is especially true in relationships. I want to be able to risk loss to challenge the status quo and have the opportunity to create what I want. I want to feel that my relationships expand my life, instead of pinning me down. I want to be able to create my dreams with another person.

I have not been able to experience a sense of knowing that I was with the right person in my past relationships. I have not felt that I could just "be," without having to give all of the time. I have not been able to feel secure, supported, and partnered. I have not had the sense that I was working with a partner toward a common goal. I have often put my enjoyment at the bottom of the list in relationships and "making it work" at the top.

Her Evaluation

When I look at my life description, it's clear that I want to be in a loving relationship. I realize that this is the only thing missing from my life right now. I also see in my description that I put my job first, and that I am somewhat unwilling to take the risks and make the changes that having the kind of partner I want would require.

My personal description sounds like the description of someone who has become accustomed to being alone. I have, in the past, found partners who are fun loving and carefree, yet what always ends up happening is that they have all of the fun as I try to figure out why I am not enjoying myself. I need some of the fun for myself.

I need someone willing to share the work of making things work so that it is a challenge we can face together instead of a battle for me to fight alone. I am realizing that I feel alone and that I have felt alone in most of the relationships that I have been in. I want a companion. I think that the passionate relationship I seek may come from building something with someone I love instead of—as it has in the past—from the intense sparks that take so much work to keep burning.

I didn't realize how much I need an equal partner. I am tired of being the hero.

You're Going to Have to Dig

Our deepest needs are often hidden from us, especially those concerning love. Not only the need itself is hidden, but also what it will take to satisfy that need. When we're hungry, we rarely have a problem deciding what type of food will satisfy us, whether it's a fresh salad or a slice of pizza. With love it's a lot more complex. When we're feeling empty, lonely, or unattached (and often we don't even know it), we rarely know exactly what type of partner or relationship will satisfy our needs.

There are three useful ways to approach our unconscious: using our dreams, using images we select, and using our intuition.

Using Dreams to Tap Your Unconscious

Your dreams can provide valuable insights about where you are going and about which parts of yourself you are working on. Dreams can reveal our unconscious by giving it a chance to "download" the events, experiences, and challenges of each day: for example, the interaction that disturbed you on a subliminal level, or perhaps a problem at the back of your mind. These are the types of issues you work through in your dreams, sometimes literally but often through metaphorical representations. Dreams thereby allow you to work through these issues with all of your attention while your conscious mind is free of external stimuli.

Dreams also present us with intuitive information that we have been repressing in our waking state. When we are asleep, the unconscious is hard at work presenting us with issues to resolve while striving to protect us from being aware of more reality than our conscious minds can endure. This often interferes with the literal expression of intuitive information in dreams.

Dreams can also foretell the future, although we're often not aware of their accuracy until later because the meaning is frequently hidden.

One Person's Example

I was walking into a beautiful hotel in Paris. I was underdressed and felt self-conscious. I entered an elevator. A man there was looking at me. I felt self-conscious about the way I was dressed and felt bad about myself. The man's name was Jon. I'm not sure how I knew that.

I knew I wanted to marry him, but I didn't think he would want me because of how I was dressed. I walked out of the hotel thinking that I'd just missed the greatest love of my life. I remember the circle driveway of the hotel as people's cars pulled out and I was on foot. I woke up thinking I had seen the man I would marry.

Her Interpretation

My original interpretation of the dream was that I needed to deal with my insecurities about not being as well turned out or as capable as others were. It was only years later, when I met my husband, Jon, at such a hotel where he was attending a formal party and I was returning from a day of shopping (in comfortable shopping gear) that I realized that the dream had no deep meaning for my personality. It was a simple intuitive prediction of my future.

Discussion

In fact, the narrator of this experience may be mistaken. At the time, the dream may indeed have pinpointed inner conflicts she was having about her sense of self-worth. I would have to see her journal at the time to be able to know for sure.

I have a close circle of friends, many of whom live far apart. We often report having dreams about one another. These dreams can inform us about one another's lives, sometimes giving us a sense of what will happen to each other far in advance. It's not uncommon for me to receive (or give) a phone call saying, for example, "I had a dream that you found an apartment last night and you were so happy about it!"

Once, when I was going through a difficult time, I received a phone call at three in the morning from a friend in Israel who had had a dream about me being in trouble. This same person actually sensed when I was in the hospital delivering my son.

Dreams keep us in touch with our feelings, ourselves, and our loved ones. They continually present us with valuable information from our intuitive or unconscious selves.

Using Images to Tap Your Unconscious

Another way to tap your unconscious is to see what images, sounds, or words resonate with you and your "romantic love-self." Perhaps you're reading a magazine and you see a picture of a person (or even of something inanimate like a house or a lake) that fills you with feelings of love. Or you hear a favorite song, a wind chime, or a teapot whistle that somehow moves you in the direction of love. Or you smell a certain type of bread being baked, or the fragrance of a flower.

These sights and sounds and scents touch a deep part of ourselves. This is a part that generally can't be accessed by consciously asking ourselves "what we're looking for." As much as possible, try to become aware of these positive emotional triggers and associations, and include them in your life.

🔊 GATHERING YOUR DREAMS 🔊

In your love journal, begin keeping track of your dreams today. Each morning when you wake up, take a few minutes to write down what you can recall or reconstruct. You don't have to go into great detail; just jotting down the highlights is fine. Be sure you record all of your dreams, even those that don't appear to be related to your love life. Don't try to evaluate them for now.

If you don't remember your dreams, write down how you feel when you wake up: the thoughts going through your mind, what your senses are attuned to, what you first notice in your environment.

Then, throughout the day, if you see an image or an article that inspires you in the direction of love, clip it and keep it in your journal. (You may need an envelope for items too large to paste in your journal.)

These images and your dreams will help illuminate both the path and the obstacles to finding or enhancing love. Review them from time to time along with your earlier exercises.

Using Your Intuition to Tap Your Unconscious

In the following exercise, you'll be using intuition to refine your love goal and to reveal qualities that will help you recognize your lover in the world.

EXERCISE 9: THE TREE EXERCISE— DISCOVERING YOUR LOVER

Begin with your body check. When you feel centered, allow your intuition to answer question no. 1 on page 75—without looking until after you've completed the exercise. (This is the "blind technique" I mentioned earlier.)

Allow all of your senses to perceive a tree. Without making any effort, allow your perceptions to begin to know how the tree looks, smells, and feels. Notice how tall it is, what fruit it bears, and what sound it makes in the wind, sun, and rain. Notice where the tree is, what is going on around it, and what time of year it is.

Now allow your tree to become a person. Who is he or she? What is his or her name? What does she look like? Where does she come from? Where is she now? What does he or she offer to the world? What does he or she want to receive from the world? Allow yourself to fully experience this person with all of your senses. Keep your eyes open as you do this.

Now allow your senses to perceive another tree standing beside

the person that your intuition has just presented you with. Allow
your intuition to use this tree to answer question no. 2 on page 75.

Without making any effort, allow your perceptions to begin to
know how the tree looks, smells, and feels. Notice how tall it is,
what fruit it bears, and what sound it makes in the sun, wind,
and rain. Notice where the tree is, what's going on around it, and
the time of year.

Now allow your tree to become a person. Ask yourself the same
identifying questions as with the first question.

Now use all of your senses to fully perceive these two people
standing together. Notice where they are, and how they feel together.
What are they doing? Can you find the love between them? If so,
why do they love each other? What are the common bonds? What
are they creating together? What do they give to each other? What
do they need from each other?

Now that you've finished, you can turn to page 75 to see which
questions your intuition was answering.

One Person's Example

The First Tree: delicate, medium height, lovely, young green branches
reaching upward with small, teardrop-shaped, bright yellow/green
leaves that are firm and shiny. It smells fresh and young and appeal-
ing; good to its core. It is a tree that is solid without being imposing.

Its scent is its fruit, and it nourishes by giving succor to all those
around it. It feels like a friend. It is part of a family. It responds and
adapts to its environment in a passionate and heartfelt way, always
returning to its calm and delighted self when the change passes.

The tree is on a small hill. The sun is warm but not scorching.
The air is moist. It is summertime, perhaps May, just coming out of
spring.

A soft, gentle man whose strength comes from his character. He
looks lovely and young and fresh. He offers solace, delight, and nourishment. Hug a tree. He wants to be recognized, embraced, and
remembered. He wants to be a part of something so he doesn't get

lost, to be a joyful part of a family. He is planted here now and wait-ing for me to call him mine.

The Second Tree: a larger, stronger tree like a weeping willow. The branches are darker and they reach downward, almost touching the ground and providing home within its branches; an older tree that reminds me of the weeping willow at the lake house of my childhood. The willows branches are made higher by the presence of the young tree. The freedom comes from the breadth of its branches and not the upward growth. It reminds me of a dark-haired Botticelli. The image of my grandmother when she was young. Heartfelt without depres-sion. England. America. Summertime.

The Trees Together: The willow's branches brush the young tree. The willow is satisfied in being itself, and the young tree is "at home" as long as the willow is there. I feel tears at the question "Is there love between them?" There is only love between them, beneath them, around them, and within them. The world comes to them and they are nourished by the soil of their past. Together they bear fruit—red, round, and firm—which becomes part of their garden. They love to open their eyes and see each other. They cannot imag-ine a world where that would not be. They catalyze pleasure for each other. The big tree gives context to the world of the little tree. The little tree gives value to the world of the big tree. They are each other's voices. They are creating passion in their everyday activities. They are bound by what is between them. In the present I feel French fruit.

Her Evaluation

It was interesting to discover which person each tree represented. Based on my description, I would have said that I was the second tree; I realize now that I was the first. After reading this I also realize that I expect to fill the role that I have traditionally filled in my relation-ships. I should explore that expectation to see if this is something I really want to do again.

I was deeply moved by my self-description. There are many ideal elements I've fantasized about truly embracing, but I have always lacked the courage to test them in the real world. I will copy my description, carrying it around with me until I feel brave enough to live up to my own expectations. My personal description highlighted some of my neglected or forgotten strengths. I tend to focus on the 20 percent of me that is not to my liking and forget the other 80 percent because it doesn't need work.

When the two trees came together, they used their history as the soil for their growth. They are happy with who they are and are sharing that with each other. Their striving is related to building a world for their children, as they already are complete with the world that they have created for themselves and the world that they share with each other. They do not (we do not) have to look for novelty and passion out in the world. It is created in our ability to enjoy what is already present in our lives. I like us as individuals and as a couple. I feel at home in this description.

It is clear to me that my future partner is older, European. This is what I am most at home with. I am going to put myself in more situations where I am likely to meet this kind of person. I get the sense that I will meet him in July.

Discussion

This exercise may give you some information to work with when you revise your love goal. Did who you were and who your lover was surprise you? How your intuition chooses to describe you may be a reflection of the individual you want to become.

Look at the lover your intuition presented you with. Don't worry if the gender is not what you expected. Instead, understand it as a symbol of the kind of qualities that you need in your lover. You can also read the gender as an indication that there are qualities of that same gender parent that you may be looking to re-create in your love relationship.

One woman actually saw a tree that her grandmother had planted when she was born. In the second part of the exercise, this tree became an image that resembled her grandmother. She interpreted this to mean that she needed in a mate the qualities that her grandmother had embodied for her as the core of her family, the one "left standing" in any calamity.

There may be some predictive elements to your intuitive image of your lover. You might want to refer to this exercise in the future as your love life reveals itself to you. On the other hand, if you're in a relationship, don't be concerned if the image doesn't resemble your partner. A different image doesn't mean that you don't want your partner. It may simply mean that you're choosing to represent your partner in a different way for the purpose of this exercise. It may also mean that you're aware of the need to create some changes within your relationship.

Examine also the relationship between the two trees. Where is its strength? Could you have a relationship like that now? What would have to change in you or your life to enable you to find or sustain such a relationship? (We'll be devoting Step Three to this important question.) Over the next few days, work with the imagery revealed in this exercise until you feel that you have explored its meaning and message fully.

Integrity: Relationships Are Two-Way Streets

If it is rare to find someone who has clearly articulated what she wants in a relationship, it is rarer still to find someone who is clear about what she is willing to offer. Integrity is the notion that a healthy relationship should satisfy your partner's romantic needs as well as your own.

A relationship is like a cell that is its own world but also exists in the world outside of itself. There are many interactions going on at once: the dynamic between the internal parts and its whole, the dynamic between the whole and its environment, and the dynamic between the whole system and time and change.

Treating Others as Individuals

I wrote this book not just for women. Men have a very hard time being loved for who they are, rather than for how well they satisfy female needs. People are not resources. It has long been acknowledged that women in ways are treated as commodities, but I don't think enough attention has been given to how men are also objectified and devalued in love relationships.

It's sobering to realize that half of all American marriages end in divorce. For any relationship to survive the many seductions and distractions in our lives, it must be win-win. Both partners in a relationship must find it compelling. The mere importance of commitment—and it *is* important—is not enough today.

In nature, our responses are driven by need. A relationship needs to be an extension of individual drive in order to thrive. In a thriving relationship, each part strengthens the whole, just as the whole strengthens the individual parts. For a relationship to work long-term, both partners need to be as invested in the survival of the couple as in that of each individual. Ideally, each moment creates both a more solid self for each person and a more solid unity for the couple or family. This may seem like a difficult challenge, especially during times of adversity—when there isn't enough to go around or when one person's difficulties begin to overwhelm the union.

When we as individuals sacrifice for another, we can be strengthened as individuals, while the integrity of our relationships is ensured. In a relationship with a core level of trust, communication, and responsiveness, a period of difficulty challenges both partners to draw on new abilities and resources. Many couples and families have pushed themselves forward to a better life when faced with the loss of a job, with an illness, or with a time of internal emotional crisis. Other couples fall apart under the strain. Some individuals remain in relationships that require them to sacrifice their needs in unhealthy ways. Those in such situations must find the strength either to change their relationship—which may involve a sacrifice—or to leave. The self-sufficiency and self-knowledge that intuition provides will strengthen your ability to do both, and offer added insights to help you decide which course of action is best for you. We will discuss these issues in Step Six.

An Ever-Reliable Guiding Principle

You won't go wrong if you always keep your eye on pleasure; in this case, shared pleasure. What do you want to do together, experience together, and create together?

Your Love Goal, Then, Must Also Include What You Want to Offer Your Partner

In the Tree Exercise (page 65), you described yourself as a lover. Now I'd like you to look over your response again, noticing what you have to bring to a love relationship. What kind of fruit did your tree bear? What were the qualities present in your love for the other person? Many of us are reactive in love. We want someone in our lives and we want that person to have certain qualities, but we give only in response to that.

Now take a closer look at what you are able to give and what you *want* to give another person in a love relationship. These may be two very different things.

For example, I am an efficient organizer. That ability, however, is not something I want to offer my partner on a regular basis. It's important to know what you want to give in a love relationship because you can then become conscious of what you have to offer. You become free to present your gift clearly, and you become aware of what you do not want to give in a relationship.

When I hear people in workshops describing what they want in a relationship, I rarely hear them say, "I want a relationship where I can be creative and enhance someone else's life through my creativity," or, "I want a relationship that enables me to provide and receive the comfort of family and belonging." Yet these are the same people who, once in a relationship, say, "I provide all of the caretaking and I'm tired," or, "I provide all of the financial stability in this house and I wish I had some relief."

One way to know what you want to offer a lover is to review your past relationships:

- What did you enjoy providing?
- What didn't you mind providing?
- What did you resent giving or feel was taken from you against your will?

Combine these insights with those you've gotten from the Tree Exercise (page 65), and you will have a sense of what you can bring into a love relationship with integrity.

Next You Must Determine What Your Partner Wants

Now that you know what you're willing and able to offer your partner, you need to be very clear about what he wants from you and from the relationship. In fact, a relationship fundamentally consists of uncovering and satisfying the needs of both parties.

How do you determine what your partner wants from the relationship? I wish it were as simple as asking him, but he is probably no more in touch with many of his needs—conscious and unconscious, rational and irrational—than you are. It is, of course, important to ask him to express his needs directly.

Naturally, discerning another's needs becomes more complicated if you are not currently in a relationship. In that case you must determine what your ideal partner needs. Whether or not you are in a current relationship, intuition provides invaluable information. You do this by using I-mode. Using I-mode, you become the other person by first allowing yourself to experience the world through his thoughts, feelings, memories, and five senses.

Resolving Differences

It would be extraordinary if what you wanted to offer exactly matched your partner's needs, and what he wanted to offer exactly matched your needs. Inevitably there will be a gap. As you come to recognize what you want, the issues in your relationship will become apparent. If you and your partner are both willing to confront and work on them, your relationship will improve. If not, you'll have some choices to make (which we'll cover in Steps Five and Six). Obviously this problem is less pressing if you are not currently in a relationship, but it is something to begin addressing intuitively.

If You Are Currently Involved

So far we've discussed what we want from the point of view of someone not in a relationship. These issues are considerably more complicated if you already have a partner.

As you consider what you want, be aware that if you are already in a relationship, that this process may make you aware of certain shortcomings. When people enter therapy and start to make internal changes (often beginning to believe in themselves a little more), they can have trouble with the people in their lives. They discover that they must allow their relationships to evolve in order to correspond to their new sense of self.

If you're in a relationship, one of the most monumental feats is to set a love goal without trying to change or manipulate your partner. This is especially true when your relationship is going through a difficult time. When you manipulate someone else, you really end up manipulating yourself. You also minimize your ability to really direct your own life in a significant way because your focus, creativity, and energy are no longer on yourself. Your changes have become directed outward toward another.

Knowing what you want in love can cause you to reevaluate the relationship you're already in. This can be disruptive to a relationship if you address its inadequacies from the point of view of being angry and disappointed. Remember that you're in a relationship because you're getting something out of it. True enslavement is a rarity. It's possible to acknowledge a relationship's deficiencies—rather than deny or ignore them—and yet be committed to working on these problem areas constructively.

To do this, you must focus on what you're getting in the relationship—the positive aspects—and on your love goal. One of two things will happen: either you'll find your relationship changing in satisfying ways—with some inevitable bumps along the way—or you'll find your life presenting you with opportunities to explore the kind of relationship that you really want.

Partners in a relationship frequently want the same thing but express both the desire, and the satisfaction of that desire, in different ways. Your mate may think that love is "taking care of things" and may feel loved and satisfied when he's treated like the head of the household. You may think that love is sharing responsibilities as well as resources, and feel loved when you receive appreciation for your contributions. If the communication between the two of you is inadequate, this gap could be a recipe for disaster.

On the other hand, many areas of agreement are often left out of seemingly divergent agendas. Your mutual desire to help each other, for example, or your shared view that the couple as a unit is the primary structure of importance. Just because he wants to feel like the head of the household doesn't necessarily mean that he wants you to be a less desirable body part. If you can learn each other's way of understanding the world, you can find areas of agreement. Your mate can learn to view "taking care of things" in a new way, while you can learn to redefine sharing.

Don't worry about this right now. Just because your current partner does not measure up in every respect with your ideal does not mean you should abandon the relationship. It is important, however, that you examine in what ways your current relationship diverges from what you want and need. Once you have identified the specific issues, you can decide how truly important each one is to you, and whether your partner is willing and able to change if you are not willing to compromise.

Coming Back to Earth

Now that you've begun the process of articulating a workable love goal, with everything that your goal entails, it is important not to get caught up in the fantasy of your ideal relationship. To avoid this danger, in the next chapter we will take active steps to make your goal a tangible reality.

Note Regarding the Tree Exercise

Here are the two questions you were answering. Question No. 1: Who am I once my love goal is achieved? Question No. 2: Who is my lover once my love goal is achieved?

Checklist

- ℘ I create pleasure and the state of love in my life every day.

- ℘ I know how to receive intuitive information about myself and others, and how to project telepathically messages compatible with my love goal.

- ℘ I know what I want in a love relationship, and what I am willing to offer in return.

Making Your Goal Tangible: Moving from Fantasy to Reality

Creating a New Reality

Once we've become aware of what we're looking for, we're often surprised to find it all around us. Have you ever noticed that when you learn a new word you see it all the time in your reading? The word was always around you, you just didn't see it because you didn't understand it. Or have you noticed that when you are introduced to someone, all of a sudden you start running into that person more and more?

Now that you've started to recognize what it is you want, you'll be surprised to find that it's not a distant fantasy. I'm not saying that your perfect relationship will materialize tomorrow (although it may). You will, however, discover aspects of what you want that you already have. This is especially true if you're currently in a relationship.

To make sure your goal remains tangible and present in your conscious and unconscious, it is important that you take the following four steps:

- Write it down.
- Create a symbol for it.

- Communicate it to at least one other person.
- Do something each day to acknowledge and affirm it.

Let's take a look at each of these steps individually.

Write It Down

Once you have begun to get in touch with what you are looking for in a love relationship, you should write down a complete, detailed statement. Writing down your love goal makes it more real and gives you a clearer, more tangible picture. The important thing is to write down your goal in the present tense, as if you had already achieved it.

Thus, for example, writing in the future tense that "I want my loneliness to end" puts the focus of your energy on your heartache. Similarly, writing, "I want to find the perfect husband," puts your focus on your search. Instead, you should say something like the following: "I am in a loving, passionate relationship with someone. We share a mutual desire to build a life and family, and we have the ability to create an abundant, joyful future together." Notice how phrasing your goal as if it had already occurred shifts your focus squarely where it belongs: on your goal.

Here are some fine, representative love goals friends have shared with me:

- I am in a relationship with a successful man with whom I share a joyful, passionate, and committed love relationship. We help each other create wonderful things in our individual lives and our life as a couple.

- My husband is my best friend. We and our three beautiful children live in a wonderful house. He has a great job that allows me to stay home with the kids. We both put family first on our list of priorities. We knew instantly that we were meant to be. We are grateful to have each other.

- My lover's passion for me and his commitment to our relationship increase every day. We want to build a life together that is full of adventure with a base of safety and creativity. We can discuss our feelings freely with each other. We are very protective of each other and of our relationship.

• I'm with a wonderful, sensual, joyful loving man, who loves and adores me and only me. I have three beautiful, joyful, loving, giving children with whom I have an intimate, nourishing, reciprocal relationship. I have mutual interests and passions with each member of my family. My past relationships have been integrated in a new and joyful way in our lives.

Create a Symbol for It

You can further crystallize your goal by creating a symbol. A visual symbol speaks to your unconscious more than a written statement.

Instead of choosing conventional love icons like a heart or a red rose or Cupid, allow your intuition to suggest the symbol. Although a heart represents love, it does so in a general, even generic, way. You need a symbol personal to you, one that best embodies all aspects of your love goal and speaks to our conscious, unconscious, and intuitive selves.

In the next exercise, you will allow your intuition to come up with a symbol that best allows you to find what it is you can most effectively focus on, in the moment, to create the kind of change in your love life that you want.

EXERCISE 10: CREATING YOUR LOVE SYMBOL

Take a few moments to become relaxed and centered. To focus yourself on your love goal, write it down once again, as if it had already happened. It may have changed from the day before—that's fine.

Allow a symbol—something simple, like a doodle—to come to mind to represent your love wish. Your journal is an excellent place to experiment with different symbols until you find the right one. This symbol will serve as a simple reminder of your love goal to your unconscious and keep your intuition focused in that direction.

Examples

- The symbol that came to me was the traditional heart. As unoriginal as that is, I see this symbol all over, every day, and it reminds me of my love goal. After a while, the heart turned into an acorn, which for me represents new growth and family. Since then, my symbol has evolved even more as the acorn has grown into a tree. Even the tree now bears acorns. The evolution of my symbol has helped me realize how much my love goal is now really about creating a family. I realized that I needed to do more work in staying in touch with my changing love goal.

- I saw a woman's open hand with my male hand within it. After visualizing the symbol a few times, I realized that when we shake hands with somebody (as during a greeting or to indicate agreement), we always shake right hand to right, but when we hold hands it is always left to right. A pair of clasped hands can symbolize both a union of equals or complements.

- I felt my symbol rather than pictured it, perhaps because I'm more a physical than a visual person. I felt a cornucopia, the "horn of plenty." I've been collecting pictures of my symbol in my love journal. When I look at them, I feel my love goal.

- My love symbol is two rings linked together. After this exercise, I soon began noticing the rings on couples I encountered. I felt very lonely for a couple days doing this. I then inscribed my name on one of the rings, and it felt right.

Discussion

Creating a symbol reminds all the parts of yourself what your main focus is at any given moment. As your love goal changes, you may find that your symbol changes, too, so it's a good idea to repeat this exercise from time to time.

Communicate It to At Least One Other Person

Telling someone else about your goal helps move it out of the realm of fantasy. This person need not do anything; nor do you have to inform this person in the event your goal changes, as it almost certainly will.

The simple act of putting someone else on notice adds a ritual element of formality to your goal, acknowledging its importance. Moreover, revealing your goal may allow others to help. If no one knows what you want, no one knows what to give you. I'm not suggesting that you read your love list to everybody, but there may be parts of your goal that you would be willing to reveal to certain people, especially those who might be in a position to help in some way.

When I first decided that I wanted a love in my life, I began asking people to include me in their party plans. The response I received was that in the past they'd always assumed I was too busy to socialize much. One lovely friend even threw a party with me in mind, inviting every eligible man she knew.

Do Something Each Day to Acknowledge and Affirm It

Finally, each day you should do something—however minor—that affirms your goal. This act can be something as simple as doodling the symbol in your journal, or copying your statement three times.

It's important to take stock of your goal regularly and articulate it to yourself. Doing so will help you continually create new patterns in the beliefs, values, expectations, behavior, and lifestyle choices that aren't helping you achieve your goal. As with all our exercises, creating a ritual out of even the most ordinary actions will improve their effectiveness.

For Now, Don't Compromise on Your Ideal— But Consider the Trade-offs

I do not mean to suggest that there is only one person in the world for you. Unless you have some sense of what your ideal partner is, however, it is difficult to know in what ways you need to compromise as a practical reality. In negotiations, it's important to distinguish between the things you truly want—the points you won't budge on— and those on which you are flexible. As you draw up your wish list for an ideal relationship, you may discover that certain things you want conflict with one another. For example, you want a successful man. You also want him to be intimate with you, and around all the time. There's going to be some conflict there, and you need to recognize that. We'll talk about how to work through these conflicts in the coming chapters.

Many years ago, I worked with a few healing groups in which people would perform a "laying on of hands" on one another to facilitate the healing process. Sometimes participants would say, "Well, I have the following seven ailments, but this is the one that I would really like to heal."

They didn't realize that the human being is a system. Everything within you affects everything else; everything is interrelated. So when you address a dental problem effectively, for example, your skin is likely to clear up as well.

That's also true in our relationships. The changes you must make to get what you want in one area of your life will affect it in other areas. For example, spending more intimate time with your significant other will probably mean spending less time with your friends.

Expect Your Goal to Change, So Continually Review It

What we have been speaking about is your *preliminary* love goal, since it is highly likely that it will change. Like the writing process, you must put down a first draft before you can edit and revise and figure out "what you're really trying to say."

Remember, too, that as you explore the exercises in this book, you will continually refine your love goal as you get more in touch with who you are and what you want. That's why we set a love goal. You may have started this book wanting to improve your relationship. Perhaps you end up finding that it has improved, but that what you really want is a new relationship. You can use this book to find that new relationship. Or perhaps your first love goal was to leave your relationship, but you have since discovered that you can improve it in a sustainable way.

If you're not in a relationship, perhaps you started this book simply wanting to attract love and to just have a great time. Or perhaps you *thought* that you wanted a committed relationship but have since discovered that what you need is a little more time to experience love and to experience yourself as both lovable and loving with different people. As your love goal evolves, you may find that you've worked through your barriers and what you really want is a committed relationship.

So review your love goal daily to make sure the messages you're sending out convey what you're looking for. For example, you may start with a love goal that stresses companionship. However, as you do the exercises in this book and reconnect with friends and other pleasurable areas of your life, you may need less companionship from your lover and more romance.

Or you may initially want a lover who will "take care of everything." As you do the exercises to know yourself better, however, you may find that you really want someone who is reliable and who relies on you and respects your strength.

Your willingness to get in touch with what you really want, and your openness to changing what you thought you wanted, is such a critical phase in your love journey that I have provided numerous examples of how other people's goals evolved.

Example No. 1

My love goal is to find a woman with whom I can settle down and create a family—without being bored. I seem to attract shallow women. Perhaps I should accept responsibility for my role in this. I'm beginning to realize that my attraction technique is to be boyish and charming. The only women with whom I'm not like that are those in my own family. With them I'm my natural self—funny, intelligent, and genuine—and they adore and respect me for it. This is the face I should present to prospective partners so that I attract the kind of woman I want, and so I can be myself.

Example No. 2

I know I'm attractive, but I realize that for a long time I've been sending out to others a not-so-subtle stay-away-from-me message. I intuit that I need to take the pressure off and not try so hard to find love. Taking this step would help reduce my natural defensive shyness and make me more approachable to potential partners. To do this, I need to take stock of all the good things in my life right now, and to encourage myself to take some satisfaction in who I am.

Example No. 3

My first goal spoke to my need to feel loved and safe. My current love goal retains these elements. Now, however, I am much more focused on finding a partner with whom I can create a loving, secure life, not a Prince Charming magically bestowing it upon me. I realized that I'd never feel secure if a relationship started from such an unbalanced place.

Example No. 4

I wanted a gorgeous, rich, sexy, passionate guy totally in love with me. I met this person before I had time to revise my love goal. He revised it for me! I now want a sexy, passionate, financially secure, emotionally stable—and emotionally available—man with whom I am in love and who is in love with me.

Example No. 5

My first love goal was about finding a man who would be a good husband. After revising my goal a few times, I realized that I actually had no idea what a "good husband" was; I would have trouble recognizing one even if I bumped into him today. I am a successful business-woman. A good husband for me now is someone I enjoy being with, and who wants to share in the responsibility of raising a family. I want a sense of a common goal, one we share as a couple.

Example No. 6

I've had such a hard few years that when I started the love program, I just wanted someone around so I wouldn't have to do everything all alone anymore. I started to attract some admirers right away, and I have to admit that it made me feel better about myself and my prospects.

For the first time, I didn't jump at every opportunity, thinking that it would be my last. I kept working on my love goal while letting myself enjoy what was changing in my life. I recently met someone who fits my revised love goal. He is funny and intelligent, and he feels the same about me.

We are taking it slowly. There are many things about him that I've added to my love goal. For example, he can find exciting things to do anywhere on earth. We complement each other very well. I am some-times so oblivious to my environment that it makes him my guide to life, which I enjoy. On the other hand, I am good at creating a home, something he did not enjoy in his childhood. He loves to sit down at the dinner table with friends.

Example No. 7

In my original love goal, I described my future husband in great detail. For the next two weeks, I noticed men with some of these qual-ities all around me. It slowly dawned on me that many of the quali-ties I wanted in a man had downsides I hadn't considered.

Initially I wanted a very successful man, someone at the top of his profession. Then I met Mark, who penciled in our first dinner date, only to cancel it because of a late business negotiation. That is not what I imagined when I wrote the description. Now my love goal is to find my soul mate.

Example No. 8

My original love goal was little more than a description of nonstop passion. During the Tree Exercise (page 65), I realized how important it was to be with a woman who can support my work and allow me to remain part of the life, friends, and activities that I currently have. I still want passion, but I also need a friend interested in her own life, someone with the maturity to be a part of my life without disrupting it. This is not a description of 24/7 wild teenage passion!

Example No. 9

I thought that what I wanted was a father and provider for myself and my two children. After completing the Tree Exercise, I realized that I'm doing all right by myself in that role. It also made me realize that *my* needs weren't being considered. The relationship between the two trees was one of deep love, passion, and commitment to each other. I am going to rewrite my love goal to include me.

Example No. 10

In my love goal, I described my perfect woman: beautiful, intelligent, a good homemaker, and—I have to admit—full of admiration for me as a husband and a man. After completing the Tree Exercise, I realized that what the other tree brought to me was peace in myself, and that the qualities in another that provided that peace are other than the qualities that I had stated in my original goal.

I think that I already know a woman who very much fits this description, and who has been interested in me for a while. She and I work at the same firm. I hadn't considered starting a relationship with her because I was so clear that I did not want a career woman. My two trees lived well together because they were alike. Although they took up the same amount of space in the garden, it was enriched and not depleted by the sharing. I think I'll ask her out.

恒 REVIEWING AND REVISING YOUR LOVE GOAL 恒

As you get more in touch with yourself, and with what you want to receive (and to give in exchange) in a love relationship, your love goal will evolve. This is especially true as you work through this book. So for the next few weeks I want you to make a point of spending a few minutes each day using your journal to restate your love goal.

Remember to state your love goal in the present tense, as if it had already occurred. Again, this should take only a few minutes. When you finish the exercises in this book, you can begin to space out these periodic reviews to once a week, and later once a month or every few months.

Continue to refine your love goal even when—especially when—you are in a relationship. Doing so will allow you to stay in touch with both the relationship's evolving needs and your own.

A Clearly Articulated Goal Releases Powerful Forces to Move You Toward Your Goal

Once your goal is a tangible reality rather than a mere fantasy, you set in motion subtle and major forces, both in yourself and in others. These forces repattern you and your environment to move you toward your goal. You'll begin to interact with others in new ways. Some of these changes will be subtle—your use of language and gesture, your behavior. The ways you express yourself and interact with others will tell everyone around you that "this is what I want."

Even without being consciously aware of your newly articulated love goal, others will notice that you've "somehow changed." Of course, now that you have a clearer sense of what you're looking for (again, this will probably evolve in the coming weeks), you can begin to approach others in more direct ways. If you're in a relationship, you will be better able to express your needs. If you're not, you'll find that other people will help you directly and indirectly.

To do this, you must communicate your goal to the universe.

What you are communicating, in sum, is this: "I am ready for a romantic relationship. This is what I want and this is what I will offer in return."

As you begin to move toward your love goal in a conscious, directed way, all kinds of relationships will begin to come toward you. You will learn to say, "This is a relationship I want in this way." As a woman, I meet many men that I'm attracted to. But I make a conscious choice about the kind of attraction I want to act on at any given moment. If you're in a relationship, you can use telepathy to send out a clear message to others that "I am available only for friendship."

Beware: A Clearly Articulated Goal May Also Release Buried Issues for You

You are just beginning to articulate what you really want romantically and in all aspects of your life. Now, the future is a dangerous place. The future does not allow us to work with any tangibles in our lives. If you allow yourself to use your perceptions in an immediate way, you can begin to change what's wrong with your future love life now. You will begin to notice where what you think you want is at odds with what you really want deep down.

It's important to lay this groundwork so you're able to sustain satisfying love relationships. I wish it were a matter of simply deciding what you're looking for in a partner or in a relationship, and then going out and finding it. But often the reason we don't get what we want is that the actual, tangible possibility of actually getting it—as opposed to merely fantasizing about it—raises hidden feelings and issues within us.

When we don't have love in our lives, we often fantasize about how great we'd feel if we met the perfect partner. In the safety of our dreams, however, we often forget about *our* reaction to that person. In fact, if we met the perfect person, our own insecurities and jealousies might lead us to destroy what we had once we'd gotten it.

Let's say that a woman wants an intelligent, powerful, successful man who loves and adores her, and that such a man has just entered her life. All of a sudden, she discovers feelings of insecurity she never realized before: "If this man is so wonderful, won't everyone else want him, too? What happens if I lose him to someone else?" Before she realizes it, she's doing things to undermine or sabotage this budding relationship.

In sum, your initial love goal may raise difficult issues that force you either to change in some major way or to reconsider the goal itself. Fortunately, you can wrestle with these issues now, rather than allowing them to arise later. We will deal with this at length in the next step. In the meantime, here are four representative examples of how participants from my love workshop handled this critical juncture.

Example No. 1

When I started the love program, I wanted a woman who would accept me totally for who I was. I met a woman about two weeks after I wrote my love goal and fell in love. Instead of trying to impress her at the beginning of our relationship, I was completely honest with her about both the negative as well as positive aspects of my personality. I let her see my warts, yet she laughingly yet kindly said she didn't even think they were so bad.

Looking back, I now realize that after a few months I was insisting that she accept things about me that were simply unacceptable. For example, I would continually promise to do something and then forget it. I was unrepentant about my faults, and I needed her to accept everything about me. It got to the point where I found myself doing things that were downright unkind.

She tolerated this behavior for a long time. Of course, my initial attraction to her began to fade. I felt like she was a doormat with no standards or demands of her own. I became very critical of her.

One day, she just had enough and left. No surprise really, given my appalling behavior. I really missed her and realized almost immediately that I had set her and myself up for the fall. I think that she *did* accept me, but the person who I had become wasn't me at all but a terrible version of all of my worst faults. I know now that I want acceptance, but I also want someone who has demands and standards of her own, someone who doesn't let me get away with things before it's too late.

Example No. 2

Frank thought that he wanted an independent woman, someone who wouldn't lean on him so much and smother him, as his last girlfriend had. When he became involved with a high-powered career woman, he suddenly realized that she was *too* independent! For the first time in his dating life, *he* was the partner who needed reassurance. He found himself wishing that she needed him a little bit more. He remarked ruefully to a friend that in his neediness he began to remind himself of his former girlfriends!

Example No. 3

Jane was going through a terrible breakup with a man who had many problems, personal as well as professional. Having barely survived one turbulent relationship, she said that her love goal was to have a simple man with whom she could share a nice, quiet life.

A month after starting the love exercises, she met a man who fit this description. Tom was devoted, supportive, and loving. For a while, Jane enjoyed him and her newfound tranquillity. Then, without quite knowing why, she found herself attracted to another man— someone in fact a lot like her old boyfriend. She justified this to her friends by saying that something was missing in her current relationship. Luckily, she figured out what the something was before getting herself into too much trouble: the pain from her last relationship, which she had yet to recover from.

Example No. 4

Paula had been adopted as an infant. As a result, she never escaped the feeling that everyone in her life would eventually abandon her. When she became involved with James, she discovered someone who demonstrated both in words and actions that he was committed for the long haul. He spoke often of wanting to build a life and family together.

Then Paula began to gain weight. By the end of their first year together, she had gained thirty pounds. Although James was concerned for her health, his feelings for her had not changed. If anything, he seemed more committed with each passing month. Then, out of the blue, Paula announced to James that she didn't want to have any children. James was heartbroken, but he reaffirmed his commitment to Paula and his determination to work through their relationship.

What's Coming Up

Achieving a goal is a process, one that involves putting together the necessary elements to create a result. By stating a goal, you begin that process.

If your goal has not been achieved, something is getting in the way. In the next step, we'll work on clearing space and repatterning your life to allow the love you want to enter it. Some of that clearing is internal and involves examining the thoughts, feelings, memories, and beliefs that may be interfering with your ability to find the love you want.

Checklist

- ✍ I create pleasure and the state of love in my life every day.
- ✍ I know how to receive intuitive information about myself and others, and how to project telepathically messages compatible with my love goal.
- ✍ I know what I want in a love relationship, and what I am willing to offer in return.
- ✍ I take active steps each day to affirm my goal.

STEP THREE

Clearing the Field

Love Byte

Removing Any Obstacles

One of the reasons we may not have the love we want in our life is that we haven't made room for it. To clear emotional space for the kind of love you want, you must let go of the past that weighs you down.

First you must learn how to grieve. We live in a society that does not allow us to fully grieve after our losses, whether those losses are broken relationships or lost parts of ourselves. Until we make peace with these losses, they will take up emotional space and energy that we need to devote to getting the love we want.

This may sound too obvious to mention, but if the kind of love you want is not in your life, you have changes to make. I don't mean you should change who you are in a fundamental way, but to find the love you want you may need to alter certain aspects of your behavior and personality.

These changes will involve both "inner" repatterning (how you experience life and explain it to yourself) as well as "outer" repatterning (how you respond to others and your environment). These two levels of repatterning take place consciously and unconsciously, both in ourselves and in others. Inner repatterning involves taking stock of your habits, beliefs, fears, expectations, and behavior patterns to see which you must change. It also deals with the hidden emotional and psychological issues that love may bring to light.

Outer repatterning involves those changes we make involving others and the world at large rather than within ourselves. These changes extend beyond those that seem to involve your love life directly. They may involve changes at work or even career plans, or the way you deal with friends.

Remember that in setting up your love goal, you needed to look at what you wanted in your life overall, and not simply focus on what you wanted in terms of a romantic relationship. Again, these are active, conscious steps. In this step you will be connecting with friends. Opening all lines of communication with this network will help you in amazing and unexpected ways. This goes far beyond simply having friends fix you up on blind dates, or finding ways to include your partner (if you have one) in your joint activities.

On the other hand, this isn't the time to be shy! People can best help you with your goal if they know what it is. You can tell them, "I really want to be in love and I really believe that I'm ready. Do you have any ideas? Could you help me out?"

You're literally putting energy into the world as you create the kind of life you want, a life that will include the partner and relationship you desire.

❦ 6 ❦

Making Space in Your Life for Love

Are You Trapped Holding on to the Past?

I'm reminded of the clever yet humane way that hunters trap monkeys in India. First they place a piece of candy in a bottle. Next they tie a rope around the bottle and attach it to something stationary, like a small tree. Then they wait nearby.

Sooner or later, an unsuspecting monkey will spot the candy in the bottle and squeeze its hand through the neck to grab the candy. Unfortunately, once it has the candy in its fist, it can't pull its hand out of the bottle. The hunter returns to the trap and captures the monkey. The monkey is trapped because it was unwilling to let go of the candy.

This method seems to relate as much to our behavior as to a monkey's. We hold on to things—objects, memories, old relationships, even painful ones—that not only keep us trapped, but also prevent us from accepting something new. Business planners always calculate the "opportunity cost" of a potential project by estimating the opportunities that will be lost once the resources are tied up in the proposed investment. Too often we tie up our emotional resources in losing propositions.

In this chapter, we'll be making peace with and letting go of the past, so we have room to accommodate a full romantic relationship. In other words, we are going to let the old go so we can openly embrace the new.

Letting Go of Past Relationships

Previous relationships can exert an emotional tug on us years after they are over. To break free of their grim hold, we must learn to let go not only of how we felt about our partner, but also of how our partner made us feel about ourselves.

Think of the last time you were in love. How did you feel different? Who did you become in it? Who did you become when the relationship ended?

When a relationship ends, we often miss not only the other person but also the person *we* were during the relationship. We miss how the relationship made us feel, the dreams it inspired, and how it affected our self-esteem. For example, if a particular relationship made you feel beautiful, handsome, or sexy, those feelings and sense of self are still a part of you after the relationship is over. The parts of ourselves that are awakened during a relationship belong to us when the relationship ends (even the bad parts). Letting go of your past relationship means claiming the part of it that is yours to take with you.

Before your relationship began, you were on a path. A relationship, any relationship, changed your path—even if only in that there was another person walking with you. A relationship always changes the parts of our life that are highlighted and the parts that are obscured.

When a relationship ends you're confronted with problems and feelings that you'd forgotten about. Often these are the issues in your life that the relationship obscured. If you look at where you were and what you were working on when you began your relationship, you can often find the "menu" of feelings and situations that you must address to find your feet again. It's impossible to be alive and stand still. You've learned things in your relationship that will help you move forward if you embrace them as your own.

You might ask, "How could I ever find someone better for me than my old boyfriend?" We tend to think of relationships in terms of better or worse. You'll find the relationship that is better for who you are right now. Never again will you be the person you were when your last relationship ended. Learning to accept and appreciate change creates the opportunity for you to always move on to something better in your life.

Act with Awareness

Once you become more aware of letting go, you may discover the subtle, often unconscious ways we let go without acknowledging it. People often inch out of their marriages in this way. Perhaps it starts with finding a job that requires a slightly longer commute, leaving less time available at home. Soon they make new friends or take up new activities independently from their partner.

None of this, mind you, is a conscious act of infidelity, but what they're doing is letting go. All of a sudden, when they fall in love with someone at their new health club, they realize their relationship is over. Because the ending was not consciously chosen, however, it's likely that the new relationship will follow the same pattern—and will probably end in much the same way.

By not allowing endings to occur, we're not allowing beginnings to form.

Returning to Complete Unfinished Endings

By this point in your life, you've already experienced numerous transitions and losses without marking them formally in any way. You probably still have "unfinished business" regarding some of these events. Because you have not formally acknowledged and made peace with them, these incomplete endings may take up a great deal of emotional space in your life, strangling pleasure and crowding out new people and new experiences.

What losses or transitions do you need to throw away? You may find you still need to mourn the loss of a relationship that ended over a dozen years ago. Perhaps now that you've achieved your career or professional goals, you need to mourn the person you used to be, even if she is not as brilliant as the person you have become. You may need to mourn slights or injustices done to you or that you've done to others.

Notice that letting go and moving on means throwing away blame and taking responsibility for our future. In mourning there is also pleasure. By acknowledging what we no longer have, we embrace what we've taken with us.

In the following exercise, I'll ask you to begin to get in touch with the "unfinished business" of your past. This is not a one-time exercise You can repeat it as often as you wish.

EXERCISE 11: CLEANING HOUSE

First, make a list of things that you want to get rid of in your life: people, problems, behavior patterns, bad habits. Take your time here.

When you have a relatively complete list, start throwing these things away. If you find there are some things that you can't throw away, such as memories of difficult times, create symbols for them and then throw these symbols away.

Examples

- It took me two months to get through this phase of the love program. At first I was overwhelmed by the sheer volume of junk in my home. Even my purse was full of stuff I hadn't looked at in months! I began by giving away books that I hadn't opened in years. Of course, I had to skim through every book before giving them away. Then I went through my papers and memorabilia. As I did this, I reexperienced different relationships and periods of my life. I had kept every love letter and theater ticket from each relationship. I had even dried flowers that had been sent to me by various lovers. I ended up keeping one or two mementos from each period of my life. I realized that I didn't need to hold on to everything. One relationship had been quite bad, and I threw everything out that pertained to that person. Going through my closets I found a decade of accumulated junk that other people had left at my house. I called some of them to return the items and renewed a couple of old friendships in doing so. The rest of it I just threw out. I now find myself throwing things out without even thinking about it. Christmas cards go in the trash on January 1. (I used to save them for years.) Even my refrigerator is emptier. Meanwhile my boyfriend has a shelf in my house—that I'm not allowed to touch, of course—for books and papers that he does not want thrown away! I am more conscious about choosing the things that I *do* keep, and I've found some real treasures in the process.

- When I started this phase of the love program, I had just moved into a new apartment that was relatively spare. I thought to myself, "This will be easy." Then I started having dreams of people who had been in my life. I spent the better part of a week throwing out old fantasies and grudges attached to these people. I also found myself becoming much clearer with the people around me about the garbage I no longer wanted in the relationship. I have a friend who is always the injured party in any argument we have. I spoke to her about this and about my need for her to be able to hear my experience if our friendship is to continue.

- This part of the love program almost had me paralyzed. I didn't do anything for a while. I didn't write my love goal, I misplaced my love journal. Unbidden, I thought about the losses in my life and had some good, long cries. Then a strange thing happened. Out of the blue someone very important from my past called. I'd been very much in love with this man, but the relationship had ended strangely. We arranged to meet. Over coffee we spoke about everything, including what had happened between us. Before we met I had harbored a fantasy that we might rediscover each other and get back together. After the meeting, however, I understood why the relationship had to end, painful as it was, for my life to continue. We've kept in contact, but soon thereafter I began to throw things out. I truly understood that if we held on to all the things and people and memories that were once important, our growth would be blocked.

- I had trouble getting rid of all the half-finished projects I knew would never be completed—the half-sewn dress, the half-painted picture frame. I was able to throw them out when I realized how many half-done relationships I have had. I want to complete the picture.

Discussion

You may have discovered that it's difficult to let some things go, even painful things. When you began to throw things away, what did you have trouble letting go of? What were you unable to let go of? What surprised you that you had held on to? Did you find, as one student of mine did, that you threw away everything? I asked her to reverse the exercise—to go through her things and instead look at the value they had.

Of course, the process of mourning need not be limited to your romantic relationships. Mourning one transition will undoubtedly raise issues in other aspects of your life.

Here is another exercise to help you escape the grip of past relationships.

EXERCISE 12: LANDSCAPE EXERCISE: PART I

Make a list of important relationships you've lost that may feel unresolved in some way. You can choose a former boyfriend, but the relationships you choose need not have been romantic. I rec-

ommend that you do this exercise in one sitting so that your mem-ory, intuition, intellect, and emotions have an opportunity to work in concert to provide you with a map.

Choose one of these relationships and complete the following questions:

1. *Who was I and what was my life like immediately prior to the time that I entered into the relationship?*
2. *How did the relationship change the priorities in my life?*
3. *What good things did the relationship make me feel about myself and my life?*
4. *Who was the other person in the relationship, and what was his or her role?*
5. *What was my role?*
6. *Who was I after the relationship ended?*

Please complete the first part of this exercise before continuing on to the second.

One Person's Example

(Note: The question numbers below refer to the questions in the exercise.)

1. I was in a relationship in which the other person was so differ-ent from me, in so many respects, that I knew ultimately it was unworkable, even though I was in love. I felt like I didn't belong any-where or to anyone. I wanted to be on my own, but I didn't know how I was going to take care of myself, and a part of me didn't care. I believed in love and that love conquers all. I felt I wasn't as good as the people around me, and that I had to be extra wonderful to make up for my deficits. I didn't know who I was or what I wanted in life. I didn't feel pretty. I had many abilities, but I didn't have the interest or the drive to work on them and see them through. I had dreams of creating a home for myself and someone else.

2. When I entered into the relationship all my attention went into making my partner's life happy and keeping him close to me.

3. At times I felt better not because my partner made me feel good about myself, but because of my competence at taking care of him. I was lively and full of good ideas. For a while I felt that my home was wherever he was, no matter where he went. I felt able to create beauty, not in my personal appearance, but in the way I was able to create some excitement about life for him. I felt like I belonged to a social group that I never wanted to be a part of in the first place, but that helped me feel that I at least belonged somewhere. At times I felt elegant and lovely and above life's day-to-day boredom.

4. My partner was a sad, misguided artist from a wealthy family. He always felt he had married beneath himself. He was elusive and mysterious. Nothing was ever enough to make him happy, and the whole world irritated him. He could create beauty from anything—lettuce leaves, colors, furniture—but he rarely experienced the joy of beauty himself.

5. My role was to keep things lively and to keep us connected to the world. It was not a responsibility he fully appreciated.

6. I felt like I was nobody and he was somebody. I felt totally without power or protection. I felt like I didn't belong anywhere or to anyone.

Her Evaluation

I realize, reviewing this landscape, that I lost my sense of belonging when I lost him. I was also the one in the relationship who maintained contact with people. I've retreated into myself since the breakup, and I need to reconnect.

I think that I need to redefine elegance according to my own values. I have an elegance of my own; it's just not as refined as his. I realize that for me the opposite of elegance is decrepitude and disrepair, as if something is wrong with me if I'm not together. It's funny that since the breakup, I've slowly allowed myself to be sloppy in front of a few select people, and it has deepened my relationship with them and their respect for me. The old questions—"Who am I?" "What am I doing here?"—have obviously reappeared.

Discussion

Notice how you were before you entered the relationship, and who you felt you were when the relationship ended. Often we put our goals and problems on hold when we enter a relationship. Then we're confronted with them again when the relationship ends. On the other hand, no one stands still, so you were most likely learning new things about yourself in your relationship.

When a relationship ends, the person we felt we'd become during the relationship ends, too, and we are left in a void. "When I was with him I felt competent and imaginative," or "I felt beautiful and desirable." We often phrase it in our minds as "He made me feel special." It's important to realize that what you were in the relationship is what you still are, even if you don't feel that way. These were *your* qualities. Someone else was simply highlighting them.

EXERCISE 13: LANDSCAPE EXERCISE: PART II

Review your relationship picture and make a list of the good things about yourself that you learned. Notice the difficulties and gifts that you had prior to the relationship, as well as the ones that presented themselves in the landscape of the relationship. List the difficulties that you had before the relationship began and the issues that arose for you in your relationship.

Create a few simple tasks to take back the parts of you that may be trapped in the old relationship. Scan the "landscape." Allow your intuition to supply an action or perspective that you could take to heal by asking yourself "What do I need to do or see right now to create peace for myself?"

One Person's Example

I must look at what I'm doing right now and not worry about the rest of my life. Whenever I feel like I don't know what my life is about I need to look at the moment and describe my life.

Discussion

Claiming the gifts as your own, and addressing the difficulties and issues consciously, will allow you to withdraw your energy from your old relationship and put it back into yourself and your life. Another useful technique is to make a list of active things that you can do to reclaim yourself and your life. Here are some of the things I do:

- Notice three things I like about myself every time I get down on myself.
- Make a list of people who are important to me.
- Have friends visit you; visit them.
- Describe for myself the home I've created for myself so that I can know its components.
- Do a little bit of hard work each day toward a professional goal.
- Devise a goal.
- Create beauty. Dance, sing, paint.

Letting Go of Old Feelings

The ties that bind us to another person can as easily be barbed wire as silk. Indeed, the angry, blaming, entitled, negative feelings we have toward a former partner are often more compelling than the positive ones.

The following exercise is structured to help loosen those ties, to make room for love by putting your attention back on yourself. Where attention goes, energy flows.

EXERCISE 14: LETTING ANOTHER PERSON GO

This exercise, which can also be used to heal a relationship you'd like to continue, may take an hour, or it may take a week. Take as long as you need. As with all of the exercises in this chapter, you may want to do it with more than one person, or you may want to do it with the same person a few times.

Your goal is to create a symbol or an icon of the person from the past whom you're trying to release. Here are some suggestions:

- *Gather items belonging to that person or items that represent your connection to him.*
- *Draw a picture of the person.*
- *Find a photograph of the person (without you in it).*
- *Write the person's name in large letters on a piece of paper.*
- *Invent something of your own to make a physical representation of the person.*

We will call your creation an "icon." Place the icon in front of you. Allow yourself to notice the space between yourself and the icon, between yourself and the other person. Allow your senses to give you impressions of what fills that space and note the information either by tape-recording it or by writing it down.

Now allow yourself to perceive the space between the two of you changing in a way that clears the space between you. Allow your intuition to provide you with the clearing. Note what enters the space between you to clear it, and what you perceive as the space clears.

Notice where your attention is when the space is cleared between you. Make note of it in detail so that you can replicate the experience whenever you need to clear this space.

Put your icon in a place where you will see it frequently. Whenever you see your icon, allow your attention to move to the state of creating space. When the space between you and your icon is clear every time you look at it, you're ready either to put it in your love book or to throw it away. Allow yourself to notice how your life changes and how your connection to the other person changes as you do this exercise.

One Person's Example

Love. Yellow, golden warmth of youth and possibility. Disappointment in myself and in her for not finding a way to make things okay. Rage at her calculated attempts to hurt me. The feeling of being devoured by her. Anger at her dishonesty. Anger at myself for the mistakes I made, and for confusion about which ones were the fatal ones. The desire for tranquillity, and seeing this person as what stands between me and calm. Years of her disapproval and censure. Anger at myself for the love and admiration I still feel for her. Grief at what she doesn't have that I had hoped to give her; gratitude for what I received. Grief for things being so bad between us that I can't say both "screw you" and "thank you" to this person.

His Evaluation

I notice myself with my feet firmly planted in my own life, not making any effort whatsoever in her direction. I notice that my reaction is that this is not what I want to hear. I want to think that there is something I can do to affect the situation besides keeping to myself. I take a long deep breath and I feel myself as separate and in myself. I keep wanting to look at the picture. I'm afraid that if I let her go, she will be harmed and I will be grief-stricken. I expect to see her energy in the space moving toward me, but I do not. It was my energy that filled the space.

I feel some pain in my heart, and I focus on recording my impressions instead of looking at the picture. I notice that wanting the pain to end instead of claiming the pain as my own and using it for my growth is part and parcel of looking at the picture. I cannot do this if I'm to stay in myself. I notice my hands and their strength in a new way.

I just got interrupted. I dealt with it by realizing that I hadn't made a strong enough boundary between myself and the world in order to do this exercise. I realize that I need to be vigilant about doing that, and to take responsibility for the boundaries that I did not set in the relationship. I'm struck by my grief.

Letting Go of Pieces of Yourself

One of the hardest things to give up is our own self-perception. Even a negative perception such as "I'm not smart" is woven into the structure of our being and is therefore read by our unconscious as a valued part of "I." What's more, all of our perceptions support us in some way, even the negative self-limiting ones.

For example, the idea that I am not smart may have allowed me to avoid competing with my friends, which in turn allowed me to be generous and supportive with them, and they in turn made me feel valued in other ways. If I were to allow myself to acknowledge that I am smart, this awareness would almost certainly push me to alter my actions within the world, irrevocably shifting the dynamics of my friendships.

This disruption is not inherently undesirable, of course, so long as I am conscious of the process. For the change to be a healthy one and not merely disruptive, I must be willing to let this perception go, and with it a piece of myself and my way of "being" with others—while never denying or losing sight of the real value these things once had for me.

Using Our Intuition

Sometimes we aren't even aware of what we're holding on to. It is difficult to let go of something we can't find, just as we can't throw away old papers around the house if we don't know where they are. In the following exercise, we'll use our intuition to tell us what things we need to give up.

EXERCISE 15: LETTING GO

You'll need your notebook for the following exercise. If you find that taking notes interrupts the flow of your impressions, you may want to record your responses with a tape recorder.

Take a long, deep breath. Allow your perceptions to follow your attention to the top of your head. Allow yourself to notice which perceptions you're having there now: memories, ideas, pictures, textures, scents, tastes, sounds, feelings. When you have recorded at least one perception, take a long deep breath and record your next perception after the breath.

Stay only a moment at each of the following parts of your body: the middle of your forehead, your throat, your heart, your belly, and your feet.

Record your intuitive impressions. The questions you were answering are on page 121, but don't peek ahead until you've completed the exercise.

One Person's Impressions

Head: I see a white sand beach, like the one I played on in my childhood. No one is on the beach, not even myself. I notice a flock of birds flying. I hear a jackhammer pounding methodically. I feel my forehead opening and everything pouring out.

Throat: I see thigh muscles banded around my throat. I feel constriction. I hear the sound of song.

Heart: I feel many balls, like marbles, so many that not one ball is distinguishable. I see nature and green moss. I see myself lying on the earth.

Belly: I feel pain and tenderness. I feel tenderness and the color violet.

Her Interpretation

Head: My concept of spirit is total nonexistence, not even the existence of self. The birds flying together remind me of a story from my childhood of lovers whose love is so strong it unites them as birds after their death. I think that I need to let go of emptiness by focusing on the eternal nature of connectedness.

Throat: I do feel constriction. I'm not sure this is intuitive. I know that, especially lately, I'm not sure what to express to others or even myself. I end up feeling isolated because I end up communicating the bare minimum. It makes sense that singing would help that constriction.

Heart: This image means a great deal to me. I think that because of the losses in my life, I haven't allowed myself to notice that any one, single person is essential to me. I am, in a sense, living according to script, not noticing my feelings. I will try lying on green moss (although it might be hard to find in these parts). Perhaps that would ground me in myself and allow me to feel while still being supported by a sense of the earth. I also see moss as vibrant and living as opposed to grass, which is dryer and less dynamic. I wonder whether the image doesn't also counsel me to take strength from what is dynamic and living, as opposed to what is past its stage of growth (like memories) and in decline.

Belly: The pain and tenderness is self-evident. I can feel the tenderness without the pain. The violet reminds me of a sunset, of knowing that the day is over and relaxing into the poignancy of the moment, allowing something inevitable to occur, and receiving a new kind of pleasure from it.

I forgot to do my feet, which I find really significant. I have ugly feet. For me, feet symbolize the attachment to the earth. I will do the feet now, even though I already know the question. I think that forgetting them means that I have to accept my own ugly parts. Maybe I'll get a foot massage!

Feet: I see the webbed foot of a duck. I see the strength of the duck's foot pushing off from the water and the power of this foot as a tool. I think that I need to look for ways that make being powerful and being human useful, and maybe even beautiful.

The Opposite of Love Is Grief

Grief may be a harsh word in the context of our love journey, but grieving is an integral part of life. (Here's another interesting fact: physiologically, the emotional state most nearly opposite love is not hate, but grief.) It may sound strange, but we cannot learn to love fully until we learn how to grieve. To love is to risk loss. We can lose our partner to someone else. Even to ask someone on a date means risking rejection.

Unless we know how to grieve, we cannot afford to take the risks that will bring us love. I will go further and say that our ability to love is directly proportional to our ability to mourn. If we cannot or will not allow loss, we are forever looking at the future with one eye on the past. Instead, we must take the past with us into the future as a source of strength.

All Transitions Involve Loss and Gain

It's easy to lose sight of the fact that times of grief and mourning are often also times of celebration of new beginnings and hope for the future. It's not commonly realized, but every time we move from one stage of life to another, we experience both loss and gain at once.

The final public speech at a college is not called the "closing" address but the commencement address. We are leaving college behind, but this is a necessary step if we are to embrace our lives as adults. Loss is a necessary part of the cycle of our lives as we grow and change.

Mark Transitions with Formal Rituals

We must fully acknowledge the loss we experience at the transitions of our lives. As with every aspect of our love program, rituals help us experience an event with every part of our being.

Each person grieves in his or her own unique way, but there are certain features of mourning that should be a part of all such rituals:

- a public declaration or demonstration of the transition so you can share it with others
- closed-ended dialogue
- an official time period to honor the transition

Let's look at each feature in more detail. Keep in mind that I'm referring to all the transitions in your life, and not just those that directly or indirectly involve your love life.

Your Transition Ritual Should Include a Public Declaration or Demonstration

The major transitions in our lives are marked by public demonstrations: sweet sixteens, graduations, engagements, marriages, baby showers, funerals. But as we've discussed, we experience countless transitions throughout our lives that also affect us profoundly yet go unmarked by ritual.

Public demonstrations create a safe space in which to experience our losses and give us permission to reach for the support of those close to us. Without such support, even the strongest of us may not be able to allow all the feelings that accompany loss to rise to the surface where we can deal with them.

A public declaration does not mean announcing your sense of loss to the world. A few close friends are enough. I cannot stress enough the importance of allowing others to witness the major events we experience. Doing so gives these events a sense of reality and place in our everyday lives.

Your Transition Ritual Should Include a Closed-Ended Dialogue

"This is over, I'm embarking on a new beginning and moving on." Too often in our mourning periods, we "talk about things" without coming to a close. Investigating our feelings is important, but without a boundary we can become engulfed by them.

Closed-ended dialogue creates a narrative with clear direction for the future. The structure of the closed-ended dialogue gives us permission to experience our feelings with the understanding and security that we have a destination.

Your Transition Ritual Should Include an Official Period to Mark the Transition

A formal period of mourning does not mean that in moments you will not continue to mourn the loss, or that your mourning will not extend longer than the period you have designated. You will, however, be providing yourself with a period of time during which you can allow your intuition, feelings, intellect, and unconscious to be focused on the task. You will also give yourself clear instructions that the focus will shift after your mourning period is over. A set time period helps your unconscious to come full circle.

Give Yourself Time

Again, just because your formal ritual is over doesn't mean all your feelings surrounding the loss have ended. Grieving does not take a moment, it takes a lifetime. However, when grief is allowed instead of blocked, it frees us to love. Mourning allows us time to release our grief and to reflect on what we loved in the person we lost.

The process of how a cut heals is revealing. Tender new skin grows under an unattractive scab until the scab, having served its purpose, falls away. Emotional wounds, perhaps even more than physical ones, don't heal overnight. I remember observing a workshop a long time ago in which the participants' defenses, their scabs, were broken down very quickly. I noticed that many people in the workshop built their scabs back up over time because the defense the scabs provided was necessary. Their "new skin" had not yet had time to grow.

If you allow healing to take place over time, you'll give yourself growth, strength, and protection. You may want to do this exercise more than once on the same relationship until you have reclaimed yourself.

Celebrating Life and Death

An Eastern sage once said that learning how to live means learning how to die. Think about that. The process of living is the process of dying. The philosopher Ram Dass said, "The pain of birth is the pain of death; and the pain of death is the pain of birth."

We're preparing to die. We don't really know what happens when we die. We don't really know what happens when we emerge from the womb when we're in there. When we make any transition from something old to something new we are giving birth. We are experiencing something new. But in order to experience something new at the very least we're transforming something. Is transformation a death? Or a new beginning?

When we're born, we leave the safety of the womb, the only world we've known, and we enter a new world. There are pleasures to be found in this new world, but we don't know that yet. Our senses are telling us that we are experiencing a difficult voyage. Then, when we've arrived, the cord that has supplied our nourishment and oxygen is cut. We feel our need for the first time. This need allows us to breathe and to latch onto the mother's breast. We begin to take our nourishment in a new way.

Ideally, the first breath is satisfying. Soon a breast is available. This, then, is the first lesson in transition—loss and rebirth—and it is a satisfying one. What if the breast is not there and we are left with our hunger? What if our cries were to go unheeded? The baby stops crying and learns that expressing need is not always met with satisfaction.

As babies, we respond instinctively to transition. When we grow older, we become more aware of the breadth and depth of our loss. When a new sibling is born or we give up the treasured milk bottle, we have a profound awareness of loss, of never being able to return to our previous state.

Our losses as children should come at appropriate developmental stages. What we lose as babies is more than compensated for by the exciting new rewards of independence. We learn that the loss of something beloved is replaced by something more adapted to who we've become. Still, it's hard not to miss the womb sometimes.

Many of the challenges of childhood involve the sacrificing of externally provided comforts to the development of our internal abilities. We learn to feed ourselves. We learn to walk by ourselves. This process of sacrificing the old and accepting the responsibility that comes with growing independence prepares us for the increasing challenges of life.

The ideal transition is the same one we made at each of our developmental stages: from womb, to symbiosis with the mother, to the healthy narcissism of the toddler, and so on, until we ourselves become adults and have children of our own. It is a complete circle. This cycle allows us to receive what we need to mature into beings who can provide for our own needs. Ultimately, it should eventually allow us to share our strength and love with others. If that circle is interrupted at any point, our ability to love, and to attract love, is compromised.

You couldn't have grown any more and remained inside the womb. Your mother's milk would not have been proper nourishment for a growing child. Had you not learned to walk, you wouldn't have been able to discover your environment. Had you not learned to be responsible for your bodily needs, you wouldn't have been able to go far. Had you not learned to interact with others, your world and your personality would have remained very limited. Each of these steps required the sacrifice of a prior state of being. Each was a death, and each was a birth.

In the following exercise, we'll give ourselves permission to grieve.

EXERCISE 16: SAYING GOOD-BYE

As always, begin with a body check. When you are centered, allow yourself to notice the first memory your intuition brings to mind. Describe it in detail. Allow this memory to lead you to others. Describe these associations.

Allow your senses—feeling, hearing, sight, touch, smell—to remember. Write down what your senses remember even if the perception seems unrelated to your memories.

List these memories. What personal transitions did they stimu-

late? It may be something that seems small, like a change of jobs, or the day you realized you were smart, or older, or deciding to change where you live.

Your intuition has presented you with a set of memories that highlight what you need to mourn right now to move toward love. What do these memories have in common?

Pick someone who cares about you to work through this exercise with you, though he or she needn't be your romantic partner. Set a special time with him or her to share a meaningful moment either outside of or in your home for the purpose of "marking" your transitions. Before you meet, prepare a "script" of what the transition was and what it meant to you. In the script you might also want to describe what you're taking with you from the transition and what you're leaving behind. Schedule this time to precede a week (or however much time you want to give to this process) in which you allow yourself to mourn.

One Person's Example

When I looked over my responses, the transitions that came to mind all involved situations of sudden change. I think that I need to mourn the loss of the safety I felt when I was part of a family. I must accept the reality that I am my own family now. I must build from there.

Discussion

Allowing yourself to grieve can create space for a new relationship in the future, or allow you to redefine the relationship you are in now. By letting go of a bad relationship in its old, outdated form, you can clear the way for a healthy reconnection.

Healthy relationships change and adapt all the time. Change is a process of loss that creates the space for something new to occur. You can't hold on to what is no longer there and at the same time commit your energy to finding something new.

Reclaiming Lost Parts of Yourself

We've discussed the loss of people and relationships and feelings, but sometimes we've also lost a piece of ourselves. If your old relationship required you to be submissive, for example, you may have forgotten your strength. If it required you to see the other person as smarter, you may have forgotten your intelligence and the uniqueness of your intellect. If your former partner made you feel sexy, your feeling of attractiveness may have left with him.

After we have let go of the grip of a past relationship or a past feeling, we will be able to reclaim that lost part of ourselves. The following exercise will help you do that intuitively.

EXERCISE 17: THE ISLAND

Begin with a body check. When you feel centered, allow your whole body—your arms, your legs, your eyes, even your mind—to become a living, breathing island.

Describe yourself. What do you smell like? What do you taste like? What do you feel like? Look like? Sound like? Where are you located? Are there any natives? What are they like, and what is their history? What food and resources are plentiful on your island? What is the weather like? What is your most strikingly lovely quality? What is the best time of year to visit? Why? What song is your island's anthem?

This exercise will be giving you information about the question on page 121. Don't peek until after you have completed the exercise.

One Person's Example

The pulse of the island, like a heartbeat, runs through me and every living thing upon me. I smell salty and I feel strong and wicked in a funny, whimsical sense. I'm oddly formed, but interesting and harmonious. I hear reverie.

I'm an island, awake and drifting, but grounded by the strong predictable pulse of my center. I see myself off Boston Harbor. My natives are dressed in white gauze and linen. They retire in the afternoons when the sun is hot, only to meet later in the evening for some brisk debate. They are transplants to the island, and they all wear hats to protect themselves from the sun. At first I was a deserted island with no indigenous peoples, but my fruits were so plentiful and intriguing that I drew many visitors who have made me their home.

When I need time alone, I arrange a storm, and the inhabitants flee the island. Maybe I should simply bring in cool weather, so that I cause less devastation to my foliage. All my different kinds of fruit have been born of that first apple that Eve gave Adam in the Garden of Eden. There is a little forbidden knowledge in each bite. The visitors come for this fruit, even though it's not always sweet.

There are springs of fresh water, but you have to look for them. Sometimes I'm no longer sure where they are. You can hear them in the quiet of the night. The water is so clear that it's almost sweeter than the fruit. My best quality is the sparkling intellect of my guests, fed by the forbidden fruit I grow. There is no bad time to be on the island. Those who stay for the storm can gather the fruits that have fallen to the ground in the peace that follows. The anthem is "Glory, Glory, Hallelujah!"

Discussion

In this chapter, you've reclaimed parts of your life that you may have left in old relationships. You have let go of what was taking space in your life, and created the space for love to enter.

Give Yourself Permission to Accept Yourself

One of the reasons I call a later exercise Completing the Positive Personality Profile is to help you get in touch with your positive qualities. In today's world, we are continually bombarded by media images of beauty and love. It sometimes takes a conscious effort not to feel inadequate in some respect. It's all too easy to fall into the trap of believing, "If only I were (blank), *then* I would find the love I'm look-ing for."

Here's a question you should ponder: "Who is the person I need to accept in order to be in love?" (Notice I didn't ask who is the person you need to *become*.) It's important to realize that you can only attract love by being the person you really are. You may not be the sultry and mysterious type. (Who knows, perhaps you are!) If you're not, chances are that you wouldn't be happy with the kind of mate that person would attract. If you're warm, open, and outgoing, the right person for you will respond to who you truly are. If you're working on presenting yourself as sultry and mysterious, your possible mate has a lot of illusions to cut through before he sees where you truly shine most brightly.

There is no such thing as an unattractive type. There are, however, certain qualities that tend to attract certain types of people. You will discover qualities within yourself you may wish to heighten. Of course, this doesn't mean pretending to have characteristics and responses that are not natural for you.

Heightening your best qualities will allow you to attract the kind of person you want to be with or to transform your current relation-ship. You'll be able to give more of what you want to give, and to stop giving the things that are stressful or unnatural for you to give. You'll be able to ask your present or future partner the right questions, such as "What part of me do you need to see in order for you to come clos-er?" or "How can I satisfy your need for closeness while satisfying my need for autonomy?" This will help you to create a satisfying and compelling relationship.

Owning Your Self-Image

Before you were old enough to have a clear sense of self, of who you were, you acquired it through the perceptions and messages of others, especially your family members. Some of those perceptions, realistic or not, remain an unquestioned part of how you and others view yourself throughout your life. By allowing your intuition to select a memory with the information you need to consciously work on, you can untangle the description of yourself you were given from who you really are. You'll then be able to find a love that is right for the real you.

Many of our misdirected goals and fears are based on those descriptions of ourselves by others that were forgotten long ago by the conscious mind. These perceptions block us from realizing our true strengths, goals, and needs and from protecting our real vulnerabilities. As you reflect on your past love relationships, you may discover that many of the unhealthy roles you took on stem from views of yourself that you were given as a child.

Revisit those memories and ask yourself the following question: "Who would I have preferred to be?" Was there anything valuable and lovable about who you were that you couldn't acknowledge then and can acknowledge now?

The following exercise will help you recognize how you adopted the critical judgments of others as your own.

EXERCISE 18: PROJECTION

As with all our exercises, begin by doing a quick body check.

When you finish, allow yourself to answer the following questions with all of your impressions—visual, aural, kinesthetic. You can record one piece of information for each question or you can write more. You may find that some questions trigger a lengthier response than others. These questions will provide information to help you answer the "target" question on page 121 at the end of this chapter. As always, don't peek ahead!

Allow yourself to perceive one specific childhood memory of yourself with your father. How did you feel right then? How would you have described yourself at that moment? Who were you and how did you feel about yourself? What were your strengths and vulnerabilities? What were you proud of? What were you secretly ashamed of? What was your worst fear? What was your greatest hope?

Now allow yourself to recall one memory of yourself as a child with your mother. How did you feel right then? How would you have described yourself at that moment? What were your strengths and vulnerabilities? What were you proud of? What were you secretly ashamed of? What was your worst fear? What was your greatest hope? Who were you and how did you feel about yourself?

Allow yourself to recall one childhood memory of yourself with your siblings or peers. How did you feel at the time? How would you have described yourself back then? What were your strengths and vulnerabilities? What were you proud of? What were you secretly ashamed of? What was your worst fear? What was your greatest hope? Who were you and how did you feel about yourself?

Finally, allow yourself to perceive one last memory of yourself as a child. How did you feel at that time? How would you have described yourself?

Discussion

Chances are, these descriptions are now actively interfering with your finding and enjoying love today. So far you've been dealing with your immediate family, but other people in your childhood such as teachers and even other children can have a major impact on your self-image. You can expand this exercise by substituting "teacher" or "important adult" for "parent."

What's Coming Up

You've begun to make space in your life. The energy that was once been bottled up in maintaining dead connections with the past is now free. This energy will propel you forward. Now we will continue the repatterning process by taking more active, positive steps to move you toward your love goal.

NB: Exercise No. 15 (Letting Go): The general question your intuition was answering is this: What do you have to let go of right now to make space for the love relationship you want? Each body part, in turn, represented a specific aspect of your life. *Head:* Which of your spiritual concepts or beliefs should you let go? What thoughts and judgments should you relinquish? *Throat:* What ways of expressing yourself? *Heart:* What ways of loving, or old love situations or judgments? *Belly:* Which ways of nourishing yourself or seeking nourishment from without? *Feet:* Which ways of perceiving your right to exist and your path in life?

NB: Exercise No. 17 (The Island): The question you were answering in this exercise is: Who am I when I have made space in my life to reclaim what is mine?

NB: Exercise No. 18 (Projection): The question you were answering in this exercise is: What critical description of myself did I receive as a child?

Checklist

- ➿ I create pleasure and the state of love in my life every day.
- ➿ I know how to receive intuitive information about myself and others, and how to project telepathically messages compatible with my love goal.
- ➿ I know what I want in a love relationship, and what I am willing to offer in return.
- ➿ I take active steps each day to affirm my goal.
- ➿ I have begun to clear space in my life for love.

⟡ 7 ⟡

Creating an Environment
Where Love Can Find You:
Inner Repatterning

Are You Ready for Love?

"When the student is ready—the teacher will appear," an old saying goes. The same is true in love. When the lover is ready, a love *will* appear.

Now that you've set your love goal and begun to clear space for it, it's time to begin repatterning your life to accommodate a partner and a relationship. This is true whether or not you're currently involved with someone.

One of the questions that most people lose sight of in their search for true love is whether they are ready for their "perfect lover." Today, if someone were to conform to your perfect ideal, would you be ready to accept him? Would you be truly *ready* for the relationship?

Another way to view this question is to identify which emotions you want to feel—such as feeling safe—and then ask yourself the following question: "Are there any reasons I'm not feeling safe at this time?" These reasons might have to do with you, your history, your character, or even your view of the world.

If you've had difficulty attracting the love that you want into your life, chances are that you are actually actively (and almost certainly unconsciously) doing things to keep love away. Amazingly, people find it easier to assume that they are unlovable than to look at the possibility that, for whatever reason (and we've discovered many of your reasons in the preceding chapters), they may be avoiding love.

The exercises in this chapter will help you stop getting in your own way. Our goal is to get you, and everything in your life, ready for love!

Consciously Repatterning Your Life— From the Inside Out

I assume that you purchased this book because on some level you are dissatisfied with your romantic life. Either there is no special person in your life right now, or you sense that there is "something missing" in your current relationship.

Again, when I discuss "repatterning your life," I'm not referring to the kinds of changes we commonly read about in books on love: improving your appearance, carrying "props" to make it easier for men to approach you, and so on. Remember that you must make profound changes in *all* aspects of your life to find the love you want. The changes must take place both consciously and unconsciously, both in ourselves and in others. Some of these changes have already begun. Now we are ready to take more conscious steps toward repatterning your life.

You actually began this repatterning process during Step Two, when you created a tangible goal. This simple step set in motion subtle yet profound changes in your unconscious and in your personality. In this step you'll be taking a look at your habits, beliefs, fears, expectations, and behavior patterns to see what you must change. Of course, I don't mean you should change who you are in a fundamental way.

One invaluable tool in repatterning your life is the ritual.

Why We Need Rituals in Our Lives

A ritual is any act or series of acts performed in a formal way, usually with some ceremonial aspects. Certain rituals are prescribed for us by social convention or even by law—the marriage ceremony being an obvious example—while others we are free to create.

Rituals need not be religious in nature. For example, you probably have your morning ritual for waking up. For me, enjoying a cup of coffee and a predawn phone call with a friend helps me ease into my day. For others, it's a hot shower or a morning jog. (Have you ever noticed that when you don't have your "morning ritual," whatever it is, that your day doesn't go quite right?)

Often the ritual itself is symbolic, such as the exchange of wedding rings. Rituals are important, then, because we decide they are important. The key requirement is the intent with which we perform them.

Our rituals can be contrasted with other regularly occurring features of our lives: routines and habits. Like habits and routines, rituals are performed the same way over and over. That recurring pattern creates comfort. The primary difference between a ritual and a habit is that habits are done unconsciously. Indeed, habits function so that we don't have to think about recurring tasks.

Rituals are done for precisely the opposite reason: to force us to think about the task at hand. In an ideal world, all of our energies are available to help us. And yet we are scattered by our many responsibilities and the demands living places on us, which dissipate our attention and energy.

A ritual automatically evokes a specific, highly focused mental and emotional state. By performing the same actions with the same focus and frame of mind over time, you can evoke the same ideal mental and emotional state on demand. This is important, since our heart will not always totally be "into it." By performing the ritual with whatever focus you can muster—your conscious intent is the important thing—you automatically concentrate your energies in a particular direction.

Athletes and other performers have always understood this, and the top ones always have rituals. Rituals help us "get into" the activity we are doing by forming a pattern that immediately evokes a certain response. Rituals are important tools for molding our reality by providing a framework to focus our attention and energy.

Laser beams are an excellent analogy and illustration of the powerful effects that can be achieved simply with the right focus. Ordinary light is composed of countless energetic particles called photons.

Because these particles are not organized in any way, even in a flash-light beam, most collide and cancel out one another's energy. In a laser beam, all of the photons have been "lined up," as it were, so that the particles reinforce rather than interfere with one another. The result is a beam that can cut through steel.

Similarly, rituals allow you to focus all your energy and resources on finding and enhancing love. The amazing thing about rituals is that they speak to your unconscious as well as your conscious mind. Indeed, rituals are one of the few ways we have of reaching our unconscious. As you perform the rituals in this book, you will find subtle changes operating on many levels that all help you achieve your love goal.

How to Create a Ritual

In every exercise in this book, I've tried to emphasize the ritual aspects of that exercise, since these help to "etch" our love goal into our unconscious mind. Creating rituals is indispensable for keeping our focus—that is, our attention—on our love goal.

In our everyday life, a ritual must be done consciously for it to have significance. Ideally, it engages all your senses and cognitive modes—seeing, feeling, smelling, touching, hearing, thinking, imagining—and connects you with your environment. A ritual must also be performed regularly, on a weekly if not a daily basis, if it is to gain force.

A ritual need not be an elaborate affair. If you're subtle about it, you can perform a ritual on the commute to work or even in an elevator. The key thing, again, is intent.

Your rituals need to feel right for you, but here are some examples that students have come up with to stimulate their thinking:

- I put two roses in my bathwater every Friday and I visualize my lover joining me in the water.

- Before I spray on perfume in the morning, I hold the bottle between my hands and I feel myself becoming the flowers in the perfume, I picture my love being attracted to the scent. When I can see this clearly, I put the perfume on. When I first began this ritual, I noticed that my perfume no longer suited me, so I spent an entire week searching for a perfume that was more "attractive," more "me."

- I fill my house with pink candles. When I light one, I imagine that the candle is my lover and that the flame is lighting his way to me.

- I set another place at the breakfast table. I also leave space in bed. I actively imagine my lover in both places.

- I make pictures and sculptures of my lover and me together. Every day I do at least a doodle that represents us.

- I danced with my future lover in the morning when I woke up. When my boyfriend moved in we danced together.

- My house was full of clutter when I started the love program. I throw out something every day to make space for my lover.

- I draw a symbol for my love goal on everything I own. I trace it on paper; I even find myself drawing it in my mashed potatoes!

- I add something that represents love to me to my love workbook at least once a day. Sometimes it's a journal entry, or a flower, or a picture from a magazine.

- I write my love goal every day and I embody it happening.

- Every weekend I make time to list the things that have made me feel loved during the week. I also make a list of loving acts and gestures *I* did. I allow those experiences to be in the forefront of my memory.

To formalize a ritual even more, you can write the individual steps in your journal. Rituals are also greatly enhanced when performed with other people, the social connection heightening the collective importance to everyone involved. I highly recommend that certain rituals in your "love routines" be done with others in your "love group." We'll be discussing love groups in the next step, but here is an example of a shared ritual between friends:

- Each week my friend and I do something we know brings the other pleasure. Last week she sent me flowers at the office. I sent her a basket of bath salts and candles to encourage her to take time for herself. We remember to tell each other the good things we notice about the other, and gently to help each other work on her weak points. We've really formed a habit of being caring toward each other. The energy between us attracts men to us when we go out together. We wonder if it would be asking too much to put "marry brothers" in our love goal!

Think in Pairs

The following ritual, suggested to me by David Rainy, a talented feng shui (the ancient art of rearranging your environment to change your life) consultant, is an effective technique for inviting a partner into your life.

Begin to re-create your environment in twos. Find anything in your home that can be arranged in pairs: two candlesticks, two flowers, two pictures together on the wall.

You Are Fast Approaching the First Dangerous Crossroad in Your Journey

You've done a lot of work in this and the preceding chapters to ready yourself for love. You'll soon arrive, if you have not arrived already, at a delicate yet important juncture in your love journey. You're now allowing yourself to be attractive to the people you really desire. But receiving the romantic attentions of others is not always a purely positive experience. Don't be surprised if the arrival of love in your life brings up some feelings other than pure joy. In fact, it can sometimes cause profound anxieties.

A dear friend of mine had been overweight her whole life. She had not had a relationship in years and thought that she desperately wanted one. Finally, she lost some of the excess weight and suddenly started perceiving how attractive men found her. However, the new-found male attention made her so uncomfortable that she put the weight back on. Unlike most of us, she was conscious enough to know her reason for gaining even as it was happening. She was not ready emotionally to be loved, and the weight was her protection.

Be Careful What You Wish for . . .

The old saying goes—you may get it! On some level we realize this, and so sometimes our fear compels us to work against what we want most!

As you pursue your love goal (refining it on a weekly if not daily basis), and begin to repattern your life, you may become aware of certain "issues" that were formerly unconscious or subconscious. I say "may" become aware because these issues will certainly arise. The pattern of our lives is built around the way we see ourselves and the world. However, much of this—perhaps most of this—takes place unconsciously.

A person may not be aware, for example, that the reason she does not have a generous, loving romantic partner is that she secretly fears being abandoned. Or she may deny herself an attractive partner because she subconsciously fears that such a person will be desirable to others and she may lose him.

Drawing Out Your Unconscious Issues Ahead of Time by Rehearsing Your Love Goal!

The problem we face with confronting and coming to terms with our unconscious issues is just that: they are unconscious! How can we logically analyze thoughts and feelings we aren't even aware of, especially when they concern situations we haven't experienced (that is, our perfect love relationship)?

So how will you react to or feel about reaching or even approaching your love goal? What issues must you confront and resolve before you can experience the "perfect" love relationship? The problem with answering these questions, of course, is that we become aware of our issues at the worst possible time: just when we get close to what we most desire!

Fortunately, by using your intuition it's possible to "try on" your ideal relationship before you have it. You do this by embracing your love goal as if you had already achieved it. That is why I've stressed over and over the importance of writing your goal in the present tense.

The following two-part exercise will allow you to suss out the issues you need to work through by using your intuition to "rehearse" the attainment of your love goal. Making your likely reactions conscious will help you to work through them.

EXERCISE 19: REHEARSING YOUR PERFECT RELATIONSHIP

PART I: REHEARSING INTUITIVELY

Begin with a body check. Once again, write down what you want in your love life as if it had already happened. (I assume you're doing this each day.)

Now, close your eyes and take a long deep breath. When you open your eyes, write down the first thing you notice with any of your five senses. Continue to investigate what you have noticed for details. You will be answering the question on page 131—don't peek until you've completed the exercise!

PART II: REHEARSING IMAGINATIVELY

Now pretend that your love goal has been realized. Perceive that reality with all of your senses. Allow yourself to view your life and its environment. How should you approach the new set of challenges and rewards that this situation provides?

One Person's Example

Part I: I notice the bars on the window. As I look out, I notice how beautiful it is inside compared with the view outside. I notice the lamp next to my windowsill and the old, crumbling brick outside.

Part II: I am in a passionate relationship with a man I feel destined to be with forever. It is evening. He is waiting in our huge comfortable bed, waiting for me to join him under the Egyptian cotton sheets. We are both so busy during the day that the night is the time we most look forward to, when we can finally be alone together.

Having found such perfection in life, I now worry that I might lose it. I need to work through that anxiety so I don't miss experiencing what I have, or color it with fears that may never come to pass. I need to be aware of what makes me feel loved so that I can remember to ask for it and not get caught in imagined insecurities. I must also push myself to continue to do things in my own life, outside the relationship, so that I grow as an individual as well as part of a couple.

Her Evaluation

The bars on the window and the perfection of my home contrasted with the outside world highlights my anxiety about anything outside, foreign, or simply different. I think that when I am happy in a relationship, my insecurity prompts me to isolate both myself and my partner from the outside world. My challenge is to allow the outside in, and to bring the beauty of the relationship out into the world. I must work on my sense of security in doing that.

Discussion

Return to this exercise daily. As you move further along the road in your love journey, new and unexpected issues will surface. Love as a concept is wonderful, but the reality of fully sharing your heart and life with another human being takes both strength and vulnerability. Recognizing and attending to this challenging aspect of love will deepen the love and commitment in your current or future relationship.

Confronting and Slaying Old Demons

As these subconscious issues surface and we become aware of them, they usually manifest themselves as fear. Everybody experiences fear. We often spend lifetimes carefully constructing a few "pet fears" that are unique to us.

Your fear of loneliness does not mirror my fear of loneliness because we are different people with different histories and experiences. But it's the rare person who actually meets in the real world the terrible monster that he has created in his mind. In the last few chapters, you have disassembled the "monster" by revisiting old experiences, relationships, and patterns of response.

In letting go, we often have a good period followed by a period of time in which our old pattern rears its ugly head with full force just to let us know it's still there. This is the moment of transition, where you see the monster in full glory and are awed by its power. It's a moment of danger and a moment of opportunity. Nothing is left hidden from you, as the monster uses its full strength to conquer the new you. Because nothing is left hidden, you can now choose to slay it completely.

Once you've faced the whole fear head-on, you'll never again be as awed by its power. When the memory of the fragments reappear, your reasoning mind will take over, and you'll be able to say, "I know you. You no longer rule my life. I am your master."

NB: Exercise No. 19 (Rehearsing Your Perfect Relationship): The question you were answering is: What issues or challenges will arise when I approach or actually achieve my love goal?

Checklist

- ❧ I create pleasure and the state of love in my life every day.
- ❧ I know how to receive intuitive information about myself and others, and how to project telepathically messages compatible with my love goal.
- ❧ I know what I want in a love relationship, and what I am willing to offer in return.
- ❧ I take active steps each day to affirm my goal.
- ❧ I have begun to clear space in my life for love.
- ❧ I am actively repatterning my inner life, especially by confronting hidden issues I may have about love relationships.

❧ 8 ❧

Creating an Environment Where Love Can Find You: Outer Repatterning

Taking a Good Hard Look in the Mirror

In the previous chapter, you learned that to find the love you want, you will almost certainly need to repattern your inner life. You will probably have to repattern your outer life, too.

By "outer" I mean how we present ourselves to others, how we behave toward them, and how they perceive and interact with us in return.

Learning to See Yourself as Others Do

We all have mental pictures of ourselves. It is always enlightening to compare the perceptions of others with our own self-perceptions. We may see ourselves as, say, organized and punctual, but the rest of the world may see us as compulsive and inflexible. I learned the following exercise many years ago in my art therapy training with Dr. Erika Steinberger, a talented professor of art therapy in New York. I promise that the results will be profoundly revealing.

EXERCISE 20: COMPLETING THE POSITIVE PERSONALITY PROFILE

On a sheet of paper—you'll find a word processor helpful for editing—make a list of positive statements about yourself that you believe to be true. List the things that you most value and believe about yourself. Your statements must be positive. Don't be bashful or humble. State everything you believe to be positive about yourself.

For example: "My eyes are beautiful." "I'm sexy." "I put others at ease." "I'm organized." "I'm a good listener." "I'm fair."

Your statements need not be in any particular order. It may even be better for you to scramble the list randomly after you're done so your list does not contain, say, ten statements in a row about your appearance followed by a dozen about your personality.

These comments should describe the total you, not just qualities you believe affect your love life. Include mental and emotional traits as well as the obvious physical ones. Be sure to include traits, behavior patterns, and even idiosyncrasies.

At the bottom of your list, write, "Other positive things you think I should know about myself" and leave space for more general responses. It would be helpful to type this list, since you'll soon be giving it to others to review.

At the top of the list, include the following introduction:

INSTRUCTIONS: *Thank you for agreeing to fill out my Positive Personality Profile. I'm doing this to find out how my perceptions of myself compare with the perceptions of others who know me.*

Below you will find a list of statements I believe to be true about myself. Please take a few moments on each one to rate it from true to very true to extremely true. These are your only options. At the end of my list you will find additional space for any other impressions you think I should know about myself.

Please be completely honest. I have provided you with a stamped, self-addressed envelope to ensure your anonymity.

Again, thank you for taking the time to complete this form. I would greatly appreciate it if you could return it to me as soon as possible, so I will be able to compare your responses with those of others.

Notice that in making your list, you compiled statements you believe to be "extremely true." Now you'll get a chance to see how your self-image compares with how others see you.

Make at least twenty photocopies of your list, saving one for yourself, and prepare stamped self-addressed envelopes.

Give one of each to people who know you in different capacities: friends, coworkers, neighbors. Be sure you ask men as well as women. Do not, however, give this questionnaire to anyone who is clearly antagonistic to you, such as someone you have recently argued with or someone competing for your position at work.

It will probably take a week or so for you to get back their responses. When you've gotten all your profiles back, use the list you saved for yourself to tally the individual ratings for each statement. What you're looking for is an overall consensus on each question—if there is one! If one person makes a certain comment, that is his or her opinion, for what it's worth, even if you don't happen to agree with it. But if three people make the same comment, you might want to explore what they're saying.

One Person's Example

Dear Friend,

Please rate the following beliefs I have about myself as true (t), very true (vt), or extremely true (et):

I am graceful.

When I speak, others are interested in my thoughts, feelings, observations, and opinions.

I am attractive.

I have a beautiful body.

I am generous.

I am creative.

I am a good cook.

I am a good listener.

I am a loyal friend.

Discussion

On some statements you'll find consistent agreement among your respondents, though it may be consistently in the negative. Realizing the points of disagreement between how I felt about myself and how I was perceived by others enabled me to investigate these areas. I could then see if they were truly areas I was strong in. If so, I asked myself what was keeping me from expressing these qualities adequately.

Notice also, in keeping with the "positive" theme of this exercise, that your respondents cannot disagree with any of your statements. If, however, many of your respondents rate a particular belief of yours as merely "true" as opposed to "extremely true," you'll know that they have some reservations about it.

Remember that it's important to interpret the responses as how you're seen, not as what you really are. The responses will help you refine how you may be presenting yourself. With this information in hand, you'll know how you appear to others. This will allow you to see the changes you could make to be more attractive in ways that you value. You may also begin to find the qualities that will help you fall in love with *yourself.*

This is important, because the qualities we find unlovable in ourselves are often the qualities we try to get others to love as proof of their love and our "worthiness." Accepting our limitations with compassion allows us to live in our strengths. This makes us far happier and, ultimately, more attractive.

Finally, focus on the space at the bottom of your list for additional comments. Did you find any pattern there? It's always a surprise to see positive aspects of ourselves revealed by others. If fifteen out of twenty people disagreed that you are, for example, someone "generous with my time," you might want to discuss this discrepancy with a friend or look within for answers. It may simply be that you're too modest with your friends about the amount of energy you spend satisfying their requests. Consider doing something to change that perception.

You'll also want to notice which of your positive qualities you and your respondents agree on. You might want actively to make these qualities a priority or simply enjoy knowing that you're appreciated for them.

You may be surprised that others perceive your strengths differently from how you perceive them. An interesting follow-up to this exercise is to create an imaginary person from the responses that you received. Maybe you weren't rated as being quite as intelligent as you thought, but you were rated as being far more beautiful and funny than you anticipated.

It can be surprising—and sometimes quite moving—to notice qualities in ourselves that others value, but that we ourselves barely notice. The "additional comments" section will often give you insight into points of attractiveness or gifts that you'd overlooked.

Whenever I've done this exercise, it's always helped me recognize strengths and gifts I didn't know I had. It's especially helpful to repeat this once every year or so. You'll be surprised not only at the responses you receive from others, but also in the positive statements you choose to make about yourself.

In the next exercise, we'll use a picture to help your intuition reveal insights into your personality and how you relate to others. When you're done, you'll give the same picture to several friends to see what insights into you it triggers for them.

EXERCISE 21: A PICTURE IS WORTH
A THOUSAND WORDS

Set aside ten minutes and choose one picture of yourself to look at. Keep your notebook or tape recorder ready.

As you look at the picture, what is the first thing that strikes you? Don't be too analytical. You're not trying to be an amateur psychologist or Sherlock Holmes. Simply allow yourself to notice what strikes you.

Record these initial impressions. Continue to look at the picture. As you do so, record everything, including any thoughts, feelings, or memories that come to mind. These impressions may have nothing to do with the picture itself. That's okay. Simply allow your intuition to present you with information you need to know about yourself.

Remember that this is a positive personality profile. If you notice things that you don't like about your posture, dress, or attitude, comment only if you can put these things in a positive light. For example, "I look uptight" becomes "I could look elegant and sophisticated."

When I was living in Italy, I envied the free and relaxed attitude of the Italian women. I berated myself for my self-conscious and restrained way of interacting. Two decades later my same dear Italian friends remember me as being lovely, profound, and thoughtful.

When you've completed this list, review your notes and interpret your impressions. Look beyond the literal meanings for deeper insights. One helpful approach is to treat your impressions as metaphors. (You'll see how one person did this in the example below.)

When you're done, repeat the exercise you did above with a few close friends one afternoon or evening. This would be a great way to use your love support group. Each person can bring a photograph, and you can all take turns responding to each other's photographs.

One Person's Example

I have beautiful white hair. I'm showing my hands. I don't look fully grown up yet (translation: I see myself as young). My eyes are intense and convey a look of passion. My facial expressions are confused (translation: I look open).

There is a large box behind me. I'm not sure what it means. I'm trying to be what my father wants me to be: creative and happy. But what I really want to do is wash my hands. I need to allow my need to be clean and pristine, and know that the creativity that my father tried to impart to me expresses itself in other ways. I feel like it was important for me to appear happy with my father when I was actually very uncomfortable. I would have been happier in reality expressing my true feelings of curiosity, confusion, and discomfort.

The large box in the picture now makes sense to me as a metaphor for all of myself that I kept hidden away when I was with him. I now can see my gentleness in this picture, which seems brittle because of the happy mask over it. I need to allow myself to express the gentleness. It will be hard. I've covered it with the happy, dynamic mask for so long. I think I'll start by making it a point to "show my hand" so that there is little for the mask to cover. I look like someone who should have a soft voice but not a hesitant one. I want to find that voice in myself.

Discussion

Looking at old pictures of ourselves always evokes powerful memories. These memories are intuitive information that will help you integrate your many attractive qualities. You can use your memories or intuitive ideas about the past to learn where your attitudes come from. This will enable you to choose whether or not to continue to embody them.

You don't have to put these memories in the "positive" framework. They are the result of behavioral patterns established by our parents and our environment that we've integrated into our personalities, regardless of whether these patterns were appropriate for us. This exercise provides the opportunity to bring this material from the unconscious to the conscious mind so that choices can be made about it.

Now that you have a better sense of both your own and others' perceptions of yourself, you can begin to consider how you present yourself. Does the language you use and your choice of clothing jibe with who you are and who you want to be? Play with the different parts of who you are and how you're perceived. Find the "you" that you're most comfortable being.

This new "you" will also attract the relationship you want or transform the relationship you have. One of the best things about this exercise is that you'll get immediate feedback from your environment.

How Strangers Respond to You

Let's now consider how you present yourself to the world at large. The following exercise will engage your intuition to help you understand what kind of cues you're sending out to others.

EXERCISE 22: RESPONDING TO YOUR PUBLIC PERSONA

As always, begin with a quick body check. When you're ready, engage all of your senses and imagine meeting yourself on the street. What do you notice about you? How do you react to yourself? Why? What could you do to change the impression you're making into a more positive one?

Allow yourself to remember a few first-time meetings that you've had in the recent past. Notice what you said, what you did, your body language, and so on. What could you have done to make these interactions more positive?

Record your responses.

One Person's Example

I notice that I'm in such a hurry it looks like I want to get away. I'm distracted, looking here and there and only half listening. I react to myself with the feeling that I'm not really interested in "me," like maybe I'm doing something to make "me" uncomfortable. It would help if I took a deep breath and look at the other person, and it wouldn't take any more time. I need to interrupt her and let them know that I'm late instead of leaving her to wonder why I'm distracted.

I recall an encounter with an older woman in the kitchen of a party I attended last week. I notice that I'm giving her my shoulder as I concentrate on speaking with another friend. I'm doing this because I'm shy, but I notice how rude and dismissive my behavior seems. Instead of feeling unable to make conversation with her, I see myself turning my body toward her and letting her make the conversation.

Discussion

Think back on the first impressions you had of someone in your life. It's very hard to change the first impression people have of you. It is the snapshot upon which they base everything that follows.

First impressions can also be inaccurate. The older woman in the example probably thought that the speaker was being rude, instead of being simply shy and somewhat inept at dealing with the situation. She then probably went on to call up all of her stored information on other rude people she had known and created a whole "persona" for this person that was based on a misperception.

Becoming aware of the "face" you're presenting in first encounters can provide great insight into "who" you really are and allow you to present yourself in a better light.

Breaking Free of Old Patterns

Have you ever left the house without brushing your teeth, reading the paper, or having your morning coffee? Your day doesn't go quite right; you feel off center. Our morning habits or patterns get us ready for the day and prepare our conscious and unconscious for what lies ahead.

Unfortunately, over time some of our patterns become obsolete. For example, we may be "hardening" ourselves every morning to endure teasing at school—which ended thirty years ago! By doing this, we direct all of our resources at an outdated and often damaging goal. This behavior may now keep people away who want to be our friends or lovers.

By consciously repatterning our behaviors, we teach ourselves to allow new and more enjoyable aspects of life to reach us. We've been repatterning our thinking by using intuition to redefine our past experiences, and to gain new perspectives on the current situations in our lives. Intuition has also allowed us to reenvision ourselves and has helped us create our target. Now we can move toward it directly and create new rituals that prepare us for pleasure and love.

You have probably already noticed changes both in how you view life and in how others view you. Now it's time to select from the information that you've received through your intuition and focus on the areas you most want to address. You may decide that you need to focus on the results from the Positive Personality Profile and try out new parts of yourself. Perhaps you've noticed that your intuition leads you to past events and unresolved grief. You may want to take time to focus on that.

Make a point to take more pleasure breaks, perhaps adding one pleasurable activity every hour. It needn't be anything extravagant. Perhaps you like yawning, or smelling flowers, or listening to the sound of rain. If you find it difficult to live in a state of pleasure, you may need to work on finding a daily ritual that prepares you for love. You can rework your life by repatterning any one of these areas. You can repattern from many different angles, each of which affects each and every part of you.

Start with the guy who works at the corner newsstand where you've bought your paper for the last ten years. Maybe you don't even know his name. Smile! Greet the bus driver as you hand him your ticket, or the checkout person at your local supermarket. Giving out good feelings will create warm feelings in others for you and bring pleasure into your life as well as theirs.

It's easy to think that we have to wait until we find a lover before we can be open, warm, and accepted. If you can't interact in a meaningful way with the people in your life now, it's unlikely that you will be able to do so with a lover.

Returning to the Positive Personality Profile

In repatterning your life, you're working on two fronts simultaneously: highlighting the positive and correcting the negative. You've been getting increasingly in touch with your love goal, and have been more clearly defining the partner you want. Now you can use intuition to highlight the parts of yourself that will help attract that person or help transform your current relationship.

Again, you don't have to change who you are. You make choices all of the time about which aspects of your personality to highlight, depending on the situation you're in. In attracting the lover you want, you will be accentuating the positive parts of your personality you want to develop further. If you want a mate who views you as an equal, for example, you may need to emphasize some aspects of your personality and downplay others.

So I'd like you to return to your journal entries on the Positive Personality Profile exercise (page 133). Review the various responses, both positive and negative. What areas do you want to work on, either to emphasize or to improve?

Don't go overboard. Focus on one specific area at a time, spending anywhere from a day to a week. Moreover, make a point of alternating between positive and negative qualities. If you have a wonderful smile, you can practice beaming at every opportunity for the next week. If you tend to hide your feelings, you can practice being more assertive and demonstrative the following week.

Making Positive First Impressions

Let's begin with the positive aspects of repatterning. What personal aspects should you highlight to attract your lover? (Of course, if you're currently involved with someone, ask yourself which of these aspects will transform your current relationship.)

These changes extend far beyond cosmetic changes such as using eye shadow to bring out your beautiful eye color or wearing a flattering dress—though these steps may be helpful initially. I'm speaking about every aspect of you: your behavior, your personality, even the sound of your voice.

In Step Two, I discussed the importance of considering your ideal lover's needs and desires as well as your own—you used I-mode to do this—in formulating your love goal. In the next exercise, you'll consider which aspects of your personality and behavior this person will most readily respond to. Again, something as simple as changing the tone of your voice may be what will attract the love you want.

EXERCISE 23: PUTTING YOUR BEST FOOT FORWARD

Start with a quick body check. When you're finished, take a long deep breath and imagine that you are your ideal lover—even if you don't yet know him.

Describe what it feels like to be him. Allow your mind's eye to see yourself through your ideal partner's eyes. Putting yourself in his place, answer the following questions from his point of view: What are you thinking? What are you feeling? What are you experiencing?

See yourself as someone he would respond to. Perceive yourself through all of his senses. How do you smell? How are you standing? What are you wearing? What are you saying? What does your voice sound like? How are you breathing?

Now discover which of your intellectual, emotional, or behavioral qualities your ideal lover responds to. Using all your senses, allow yourself to perceive who your perfect lover reacts to with desire, love, respect, and caring.

Examples

- When I put myself in this man's place, I notice what is visual in my environment. I think about buildings and architecture; I feel a part of the physical and architectural structures of my environment much more than I do the people in it. The only exception seems to be the people I consider to be family. I experience the world as foreign and out of control, which is why I like the conventions of polite society and traditional business. I am creative within those conventions.

- I would respond to a woman who is both eclectic and eccentric yet socially conventional. I like creativity and originality "contained," for lack of a better word, by good behavior. I like slow conversation, with enough space between words for calm reflection. I want to be the one to ask to meet again or to make the first call. I actually decide how I feel and what my intentions are toward another person almost immediately, but it takes a while for the other person to respond in kind, and I do not like to be pushed at someone else's speed or sense of urgency. I usually get what I want, and I admire and am drawn to others with that same strength and determination.

- My breathing feels slow, like that of someone asleep. Through my lover's senses, I smell warm but not overly sweet or scented. I am standing somewhat apart from the group but not aloof. I am wearing a narrow black skirt and pumps, very elegantly dressed all in one color. At first, I respond briefly to his conversation. Then I speak about an interesting place I'd visited a few weeks ago, pointing out especially the golden light in one of the buildings there.

- My lover responds to my quiet shyness, and to how deeply I interact with and feel everything around me. He respects and admires the way I take strength from the presence of others, and the discreet way I offer support to those dear to me. He also admires my ability to allow someone else to lead, taking what I need out of an experience while offering my input unobtrusively. He likes the way I stroke the fabric of the couch as I speak. He loves the way I enjoy all things tactile: food, fabrics, lips. He accepts and even loves my little pockets of stubbornness, hidden so expertly until someone bumps up against one of them. He loves how I feel in his arms, full and fragile at the same time.

Discussion

Now you have intuitive information about the kind of person your ideal lover is looking for, or the kind of person you would be in your ideal relationship. Work on these qualities in the coming weeks. High-light these aspects one at a time, experimenting with different ones in different situations, or you can try to bring them all to the forefront immediately.

Again, please understand that I'm not saying you should change the fundamental "you." Nor are you "pretending" to be anything or anyone other than who you are. All I'm talking about is presenting yourself in the best possible light. How you do this will of course vary, depending on the nature of your love goal.

You may want to repeat this exercise when you're going into situations in which you're likely to meet people. The following exercise will allow you to know which aspects of you should be highlighted in whatever situation you find yourself.

How to Make an Immediate Impression on Someone Using Intuitive "Quick Hits"

Intuition is especially useful in situations where you need to react quickly and appropriately. Remember that intuition's job as a survival skill is to give you the information you need—especially when you don't have time to plan ahead or think clearly.

The following exercise will help you in such interactions.

EXERCISE 24: MAKING POSITIVE FIRST IMPRESSIONS

The next time you're in a social setting, focus on your goal. This might be as simple as "How can I create a positive bond between myself and that individual across the room right now?"

With that in mind, do a quick body check, perhaps for a second or two. What is the first perception you receive? Interpreting this impression will give you insight into what you should highlight— or even what you should be aware of—to make the encounter a positive one.

One Person's Example

During my body check, I realize that I am all over the place, with a million thoughts and things to do. I can't focus. I get the sense that I must allow myself to sink into my exhaustion instead of fighting against it to keep up my flagging and scattered energy.

My goal is a good connection with Kevin, my boyfriend's childhood friend, whom I'm about to meet for the first time. I ask my intuition what part of me to lead with to connect with this person in a positive way so he will support my relationship with my boyfriend. I see myself carrying a book and being somewhat reserved.

The Result

When I met Kevin, I liked him immediately. After a few polite exchanges, the guys started in on an "old times" conversation, and I opened my book and let them talk. I needed the rest, and they needed the time together. If I hadn't had a book with me I think that I would have gotten annoyed, and the camaraderie of the meeting, which I ended up being a comfortable part of, would have been disrupted.

Discussion

Your "quick hits" will give you an opening or a direction that you can add to the other information available to enable you to make better contact or to respond in a more positive way to potentially difficult situations.

Getting Your Life in Order

What I'm really talking about, then, is the importance of getting *all* aspects of your life ready for love. Since I'm talking about the future—and possibly someone you have not even met!—this is a difficult matter to approach logically. Moreover, as you well know by now, in repatterning your life, you may be approaching unconscious or subconscious issues.

Fortunately, our intuitive faculties are especially suited for just this kind of task. This will become clear in the following exercise, which puts together all the issues we've been addressing in this chapter.

EXERCISE 25: PUTTING YOUR HOUSE IN ORDER

In a moment, I will ask you to allow your intuition and imagination to perceive and describe a house, drawing on all of your senses. Feel free to record your impressions with drawings as well as words.

As you continue this exercise, I will provide questions to prompt you. Please note that these questions are not meant to cover everything your intuition may suggest. Don't try to respond logically to the questions. Instead, simply allow your intuition to speak. Remember that your impressions may not seem to make sense or even to address the question you're considering.

Finally, make sure to complete the first part of this exercise before beginning the second. In other words, do not peek ahead!

PART I: RECEIVING YOUR IMPRESSIONS

Take a long, deep breath and do a quick body check. Allow your mind and every muscle in your body to relax.

When you're ready, allow yourself to imagine that there is a house in front of you at a distance. Use all of your senses to describe this house in as much detail as you can. As you do so, consider the following questions:

- *What season is it?*
- *How far away is the house?*
- *Where is it?*
- *What are its colors?*

In a moment, you will begin to walk toward the house. On the way there, you may encounter some situations. Some may be pleasant, but some may be difficult.

- *What do you need to wear?*
- *What do you need to carry?*

Now begin your journey toward the house.

- *Do you encounter anyone or anything along the way? If so, how do you respond?*
- *How does the house begin to look different as you near it?*
- *How many doors does it have? Windows?*
- *What does it smell like?*
- *What is the house made of?*
- *What surrounds the house?*
- *Who does this house remind you of?*

Now describe how you enter the house, and how you feel once you're inside.

- *How do you enter the house: front door, back, window?*
- *Who lives in the house? Does he or she greet you? Do you sense any names?*
- *How many rooms does the house have?*
- *What does it smell like when you are inside? Do you hear any sounds?*
- *What is the first room that you go to?*
- *Does it remind you of anyplace? Any person?*
- *How is the house laid out?*
- *Where in the house do you want to go?*
- *Does anybody live in the house?*
- *Do you want them there?*
- *What would you want to change in the house to make it more comfortable?*
- *What do you love about this house?*

Before you settle into the house, you may need to make certain changes or adjustments. Record these.

Allow yourself to know that this house belongs to you, and that you will always live within it. How do you react to or feel about that idea?

When you have completely described your experience of the journey toward the house and the house itself, you can begin Part II.

PART II: INTERPRETING YOUR IMPRESSIONS

The following guidelines will help you interpret your intuitive impressions. Again, don't read any further until you have completed the first part.

- *The house at a distance represents what you're currently moving toward in your love life.*
- *What you need to bring with you represents what you need to acquire or address in order to reach your love goal.*
- *What you need to wear represents the parts of your personality or behavior that you need to emphasize.*
- *What you need to carry represents what you need to be aware of in order to attract love.*
- *Everything you encounter represents past experiences that you need to consciously work through to reach your love goal. (However, if you encounter someone you don't know, it may be your future mate!)*
- *The distance between you and the house represents the distance between you and your love goals. If they are too far, you may want to do some intuitive work on how to bring them closer more quickly.*
- *The house up close represents the reality of what your love goal is for you. If you don't like the house up close, you might want to do some extra intuitive work on your love goal.*
- *The entrance represents how you approach your love goal. Interpreting the entrance to your house will help you see what makes it easier or more difficult for you to attract a love relationship. If you find the doorway difficult or unpleasant to enter, you might want to do some extra intuitive work on*

negotiating the insecurities you have around being in a love relationship.

- *The reminiscence you have of a person or place tells you something about your partner or future partner.*

- *The layout of the house gives you some information about the structure of your relationship or future relationship.*

- *Where in the house you want to go (the basement, the top floor) has many possible interpretations, such as the purpose you need the relationship to serve, or what you focus on in relationships. Look carefully at this exercise and allow it to reveal to you where you keep yourself when you are in love.*

- *If someone from the past lives in the house with you, ask yourself why that person is there and whether he or she belongs. If you don't recognize the person, he may be someone you have yet to meet.*

- *The changes you would make in your house represent the changes you might want to consider in your love goal or relationship.*

One Person's Example

At first I'm in the house, an airy Mediterranean house with huge doors and windows. I then remember that I'm supposed to see the house at a distance. I see it at the bottom of a small hill. It's a house that I know from my childhood, but warmer and more inviting. I keep thinking that I don't really want this house, but it keeps appearing anyway. It's made of wood and modern brick and is at the bottom of a steep, perilous driveway.

To reach the house safely, I need to know that the house is different from what it was in its former life (my life). I need to bring my experience and also a sense of distance. I need to go alone so that my attention is focused only on myself.

I need to wear something soft and comfortable. I don't need to be pretentious. I need to wear something that allows me to express my own natural electricity, passion, and joy.

I need to carry a bag containing my own bottle of water, a few snacks, my soap, and anything else I need for comfort. I need to carry these things by myself, so the bag shouldn't be too heavy. It should be a shoulder bag or backpack so that it leaves my hands free.

I begin my journey and am already there, as though returning to a place I once knew. I see myself as young and fresh, but now I'm wise. I see a young version of myself in blue jeans and a T-shirt. This young version is bronzed and watching, as if she has always known I would eventually return.

The house turns white as I approach it. It has fragrant vines and flowers around the door, which is bright, fresh, and golden, almost Arabic. I see now that it extends farther back than I thought.

The entrance pulls me in. I feel immediately at home. I'm also very tired, but my exhaustion turns quickly into a sense of relaxation as I settle into a little corner chair at the entrance.

The house appears to be all on one level, but I know that the old house, the house of my youth, is below it. Now I see steps going up. As I follow them, I see many light rooms bordered by a veranda.

I want to be in these upper rooms. I want to lay myself down on one of the beds and feel the breeze from the door windows, the warm humid breeze floating over me as I sleep.

I can hear children playing in the next room. They are my children, but I know that they are cared for, so I can take this time to rest.

I wouldn't change anything in this house, although I might want the lower level, the level from my past, to disappear completely.

I love everything about this house. I can now feel my entire family coming to visit. There is space for them.

I take the lower level of the house away and I realize that it was only a figment of my imagination. This house is not built on the old one. It's built by the faith of the little girl sitting high in the tree.

I want to grow old in this house. I want it always to be a place of comfort for my family to visit. I want this house now.

Discussion

Which questions did you answer? Which did you ignore? Perhaps you answered questions I didn't even ask! This is simply your intuition's way of highlighting the most important issues for you as you proceed in your love journey.

Take time to interpret your information in as much depth as you can. Review this exercise frequently over the next few weeks. When your relationship or relationship status changes, do this exercise again. This time, integrate into the exercise your new situation, your new intuitive information, and your intuitive information about the needs of your mate. If you're not currently involved, repeating this exercise when you're in a relationship will allow you to combine what is harmonious about both you and your partner's "love home."

By the way, there is nothing magical about the house. It was simply a symbol I chose to give your intuition a chance to speak rather than your logical mind.

The purpose of the preceding exercise was to allow your intuition to provide insights that will help guide your repatterning efforts. Remember that your logical, analytic mind can give you insights, too.

So what areas of your personality, behavior, or life do you need to repattern? Don't expect to answer this immediately. Use your journal to record your insights in the days and weeks ahead.

What's Coming Up

Now that you've begun the process of actively repatterning your life to accommodate love, it's time to reconnect with the other important relationships in your life: your friends. Intuitive training teaches us that we are connected to everyone and everything, to events we don't know and to people we haven't yet met. Our awareness of this "connectedness," and especially our connection with our friends, has great power to support life, growth, and the journey toward love.

Checklist

- ᐱ I create pleasure and the state of love in my life every day.

- ᐱ I know how to receive intuitive information about myself and others, and how to project telepathically messages compatible with my love goal.

- ᐱ I know what I want in a love relationship, and what I am willing to offer in return.

- ᐱ I take active steps each day to affirm my goal.

- ᐱ I have begun to clear space in my life for love.

- ᐱ I am actively repatterning my inner life, especially by confronting hidden issues I may have about love relationships.

- ᐱ I am actively repatterning my outer life, examining intuitively and otherwise the ways I present myself and interact with others.

STEP FOUR

Finding the Garden of Eden

Love Byte

Reconnecting with the Other Relationships in Your Life

In the previous step, you began the process of actively repatterning your life to accommodate love and a lover. Now it's time to return to the other relationships in your life, particularly your friendships. When we pursue a romantic relationship, or we already have one, there is a strong tendency to let our friendships take second place. Naturally a romantic relationship has special demands once we commit ourselves, but it is important not to abandon our friends.

Romantic relationships, while different from our other friendships, are not as different as people imagine. They both present similar rewards and challenges. Maintaining your friendships requires that you use and develop many of the same positive qualities and relationship skills—sharing, honesty, empathy, listening, communicating—as a romantic relationship does. We can look at it this way: someone who has difficulty with her friendships will certainly have difficulties in her romantic relationship, which is the most important one of all.

One way to work through these issues is to form a love support network. A support network (or group) is a microcosm of relationships that provides you with a safe environment to work out difficulties you may face while repatterning your life to accommodate love. Members can express themselves and receive supportive feedback from others who care about them. Moreover, members can share their resources and contacts with one another.

❧ 9 ❧

Reaffirming Your Friendships and Other Meaningful Relationships

The Second Crossroads: Reconnecting with Your Friends

You'll recall that the first crossroad we face in our love journey involves the issues that come up when we have a satisfying relationship in our lives, or even when we begin to approach a relationship. Without cultivating our awareness of these issues intuitively and through other means, we often sabotage promising romances.

We now come to the second crossroad. While we have been traveling together on our love journey, we don't want to lose sight of our friendships. Relegating our friends to second place is an especially strong temptation for both those looking for love and for those who have found it.

When looking for love, we often become so focused on what we want romantically that we put all our energy into our love goal and sometimes ignore our friends altogether. Moreover, in times of loneliness, we sometimes shy away from social contacts and insulate ourselves, perhaps because we are unwilling to burden our friends with our problem.

And when we find the love we want, we often "cocoon" with our partner, cutting ourselves off from "the outside world." This is a natural urge at the beginning of a relationship. Yet while a romantic relationship places special demands on our time and attention, we should be careful to never overlook our friends.

Romantic relationships, while different from our other friendships, are not really as different as many people imagine. And since you most likely want your lover to be your best friend, friendships are an excellent place to work on our "relationship skills." Especially when you are looking for the ideal partner, it's important to connect to the web of caring and pleasure that friendship provides, as well as to negotiate the challenges it presents.

Maintaining a friendship requires many of the same positive qualities as maintaining a romantic relationship, and presents many of the same challenges. We can look at it this way: someone who has difficulty with her friendships will certainly have difficulties with her most important one—her romantic relationship.

The Enduring Value of Friendship

Numerous scientific studies have established beyond doubt that people who have satisfying friendships and romantic relationships live longer, healthier, more resilient lives. If you are not yet in a deeply fulfilling romantic relationship, your friendships are especially important. Friendship keeps you connected to a caring community of people, while helping prepare you for your future romantic relationship. It can also give you insights into a current love relationship.

Friendships can endure over decades, even lifetimes, supporting us in difficult times and sharing joyous times with us. Friends form a part of our adult family. They celebrate, mourn, and witness our life and its changes. I have a friend from almost every period of my life, from nursery school through the present. Although the particular attributes I chose each person for reflected who I was at the time, all my friends have basic values and ways of responding in common with me. Even my best nursery school friend, Jean, still embodies, these decades later, many of the qualities I admire most.

Your greatest support in your love journey is your network of friendships. If you don't feel that you have friends in your life and you want them, look hard, because potential friends are all around you wanting what you have to offer and offering what they have to share.

Each Friendship Allows Us to Experience Another Part of Ourselves

There's an old saying that we live a different life for every language we speak. The same may be said of friendships. No two of our friendships are exactly the same. Each one reflects a different aspect of our personality.

Expecting our partner to be everything to us ruins many a relationship. Friendship provides us with things that may be missing in our partner, and can relieve our partner from playing roles he is unsuited for. In both love and friendship, we admire both the other person and our reflection in his or her eyes.

Think of a few of your friends. Then think of "who" you are with them. You accent and enjoy different aspects of yourself with different people, as they do with you. Friendship allows you to have broad tastes and to continue to grow, cultivating and enriching the many sides of your personality.

Friendship Is a Learned Art

You often hear people say they are "working on" their romantic relationships, yet you rarely hear that said of friendships. Our friends aren't perfect. Neither are we. Friendship, like any other relationship, has its ups and downs. Any long friendship will have moments of doubt. Indeed, friendships have many of the pitfalls and trials that romantic relationships do. Conflicts between friends tend to be less entangled and more easily resolved than are those between lovers. This is partly because friendships do not usually take place in the intense space of a monogamous relationship. But the resonance that motivated your choosing that friend is something to be treasured.

Learning how to work through both the good times and bad times in friendship will help prepare you for your love relationship. We will discuss working through difficulties in great detail in Step Five.

Learning Just to Listen

A big part of being a friend is, of course, listening. I don't mean simply hearing the person's words. I mean listening with all of your senses, not only to what is said, but also to what *isn't*. When you develop the skill of intuition, you develop the ability to listen to information from yourself and from your environment that you may have been ignoring. This is an important skill in love.

We tend to listen with our logical minds, analyzing what the person is saying so we can offer reassurances or solutions. This is especially true of men. Try listening with your intuition, offering not reassurance or solutions but rather your presence and empathy. People are often deeply touched and helped when they simply feel heard without being solved, or when their experiences are not immediately related to one of your own.

Try the following experiment for a week: the next time someone close to you is trying to express something to you, do a body check. As you do the body check, notice to what degree your senses are following what the person is attempting to communicate. Also be aware of what the person is not saying. Just listen.

This is one of the most powerful ways I know of connecting with another person. Learning to listen to others, whether they're your friends or strangers, will help you listen to your lover. And when you learn how to listen to others, you make it that much easier for others to listen to you.

Checklist

- ♲ I create pleasure and the state of love in my life every day.
- ♲ I know how to receive intuitive information about myself and others, and how to project telepathically messages compatible with my love goal.
- ♲ I know what I want in a love relationship, and what I am willing to offer in return.
- ♲ I take active steps each day to affirm my goal.
- ♲ I have begun to clear space in my life for love.

⨎ I am actively repatterning my inner life, especially by confronting hidden issues I may have about love relationships.

⨎ I am actively repatterning my outer life, examining intuitively and otherwise the ways I present myself and interact with others.

⨎ I reaffirm my friendships and other meaningful relationships, and I continually practice my relationship skills.

❦ 10 ❦

Building a Support Network to Help You on Your Journey

Creating a Community

Friendship is the connection between people who care for each other. Community, on the other hand, is the connection among people who care about and work toward a common goal. A love support group is a community that can help you in many important ways, including the following:

- It pools resources and contacts for its members to share. Members of love groups become very generous as they get to know one another. The energy of a group is far greater than the sum of its parts. You can tap not only the talents and ideas of each individual member but also the "synergy" released by the collective network. By joining an intuitive love group, you can offer what you can—an ear, a shoulder, a hug, maybe even your old wardrobe—and receive what you need within an enduring community.

- It provides a positive, nurturing environment. A support group provides you with a safe environment in which to work out any difficulties you may face while repatterning. Members can express themselves freely and receive supportive feedback from others.

- It allows you a framework to practice your listening technique. Try the following group exercise. As each person says something, the others can practice being present with all of their senses. Later, they can mirror back to the speaker that they have understood the importance of what the speaker expressed.

As the members of the group share pleasure together and begin to see how much the energy of the group has contributed to love entering their lives, a community forms that is open and supportive. Of the many types of groups I have led and participated in, I have found the most sharing of resources, ideas, and caring among the love groups.

Form a Support Network Even If You Are Already Involved

You can form a love group in many ways. Post a sign-up sheet at your local bookstore. Ask your friends to join you in finding a relationship, or improving the one they have. Perhaps you'll find members on the Web, with its tens of thousands of interest groups.

Not every group member has to be a close friend. I strongly recommend, however, that any love support group confine itself to members who are seeking a relationship with one sex only, whether male or female. These may be enlightened times, but the sensitive issues addressed in love support groups would be needlessly complicated by the tension produced by potential romantic possibilities within the group. (Having said that, I just realized that given today's various relationship possibilities, members' gender preference rather than their sex might be the important factor!)

Your love group will not only provide you with the help of other human energy working toward a similar goal but also with the resources of each member to help you toward your goal. But remember that love groups, like your friends, are not just a means to an end, to be abandoned once you are romantically involved. Your love group is a network of friends and support that will provide a community for the rest of your life for yourself and your relationship.

Groups Dynamics Create Powerful Transformations

Your experience in a group can profoundly affect your ability to exchange old patterning for new ways of behaving. This, in turn, will help clear the path of your love life.

One of the first love groups I ever held was comprised almost entirely of teachers and leaders in their respective fields. Each person arrived prepared with the first series of exercises in this book completed; two had already had results in their love life from their hard work.

I had structured an opening ritual for the group. We all stood in a circle. I lit a candle and passed it around, beginning with the person on my left. As each person held the candle, she stated her love goal and the image that represented that goal. After the last person returned the candle to the first, I asked the group to imagine that we were a circle of loving family, if only for an evening, and to focus on how we could all help one another.

We then planned to do a little prediction and share our intuition with one another about aspects of our goals that needed work. As we progressed, it turned out that two people in the group were neither teachers nor leaders. It immediately became apparent to everyone that we were focusing our attention on these two people.

Almost simultaneously, we all became aware that we were so unaccustomed to receiving guidance and help from others that we had to focus on helping those we perceived as "students" instead of being open and receiving for ourselves. We immediately restructured the time, realizing that it was that exact quality that was interfering with our ability to create supportive love relationships for ourselves. The "students" realized that they, too, had something to offer and that their student role was a roadblock to their finding relationships where they were valued and their contributions were respected.

Shedding our everyday roles, if only for an evening, was liberating for everyone. The "students" gave some great feedback as the "teachers" found themselves receiving help and learning to ask for it. One woman (one of the "students") had her first date in eleven years the following week. Although she liked the man, for the first time she felt no sense that this was her last chance. Trusting her intuition, she was able to discern that this man would make a nice friend but not a good partner. Indeed, two weeks later she had another date with someone who was more her type. For the first time, she was able to allow the relationship to develop naturally, instead of clinging to it right away.

Another group member had been in a relationship for some time. He and his partner had been contemplating marriage (mostly his partner). Over the past year, he'd grown less satisfied with different aspects of her and was unsure that she was the right person for him. He didn't feel that she really gave him very much, although he enjoyed her and had a great deal of respect for her as a person.

That evening, he realized how uncomfortable accepting things from others made him feel, and how difficult he made it for others to give him anything. In the Putting Your Best Foot Forward exercise (page 143), he felt his partner's feelings from her point of view and was very moved by her genuine desire for his happiness and well-being. In the following weeks he started relating to his partner in a different way. He tried allowing her to lead more of the time. He discovered that he received more of what he needed when he let his partner take charge sometimes than when he insisted on structuring their lives and being the teacher.

How to Conduct Your Group's Meetings

Group meetings should not be aimless get-togethers, but neither should they be completely structured. Your group should meet regularly—at least once a month—though how your group holds its meetings will vary, depending on your particular group dynamics as well as on how everyone is feeling on that particular day. Keeping in mind that pleasure chemicals are released with laughter, I offer the following general points as guidelines:

- A good group format begins with an opening exercise to bring the group together, such as each member introducing herself and speaking about what is most important for her at that moment. You can discuss your goals, what has happened since the last meeting, what you hope to take away from the meeting, difficulties, hopes and dreams, and so on.

- Do something to get the energy and connection moving. This could be anything from saying tongue twisters as a group to dancing to a song together, to partnering for foot massages.

- State the goal of the evening. You can follow the outline of this book or you can jump around, for example starting with "letting go of family and friends." You can also create experiences or exercises of your own to do as a group.

- Do an exercise, trade individual readings, or even do group readings. I'll show you how shortly.

- Do something pleasurable together such as telling jokes, sharing food, or even going out together to a restaurant or movie.

- End with a closing exercise. This could entail each person stating her love goal to the group or giving every other person in the group an intuitive love symbol, prediction, or some feedback.

Again, these are general guidelines. Experiment with different variations. You may want to return to our earlier discussion of rituals to give you further ideas. Here is an example of how one person's group conducts its meetings.

One Person's Example

Our group gets together on the full moon every month (which seems a more natural and romantic rhythm than meeting on "the last Sunday of every month"). The group started when a few of us from the love workshop wanted to continue to meet. Once we got started, members brought friends.

For each meeting, everyone prepares something symbolic to give to the others to help them find and enhance love. One person brought a heart-shaped soap for each person and wrote a morning bathing ritual for everyone to perform each day.

Another brought some beautiful fabric and instructed us to sew a pillow, seeing our stitches as bringing our partner into our life. She gave us some cotton and jasmine blossoms to start us off. The ritual was to add things to the stuffing over the next month that represent love to us. We all picked a specific time to sew the final seam so each of our good wishes would be part of the pillow at the same moment.

A couple of members who have been partnered since the beginning still attend regularly; one even brought in his partner—something we don't usually do—to keep the love in their relationship. The one man in our group created an interesting ritual. He told us each to bring a shoe box to the next meeting. He brought glue and Popsicle sticks and tiny paintbrushes and model paint. He told us to build our home with our lover in it with us, and to add things to this home over the next month. Perhaps it worked—two of us fell in love that month!

Sometimes people just bring token gifts. One person brought a basket of sensual fruit; another brought a tape of love songs for each of us to listen to each day. As the group has expanded, the old-timers (the people who attended the first meeting) lead the rituals while the newcomers bring gifts. Sometimes we have a group leader, depending on how we all feel.

A Short Course in How to Give a Reading

As I mentioned earlier, giving group readings is a particularly useful function of love support groups. Members can pair off and give readings to each other one-on-one, or the group can collectively give a reading to one particular member. I'll show you how to do both.

In chapter 2, "A Crash Course in Using Your Intuition," we discussed how to access intuition, so by now you should be well acquainted with how to give readings for yourself. Giving readings for someone else is very similar, but there are some key differences, too.

Begin with a body check. Allow yourself to notice all of your senses. Allow them to create a story for your "target," starting with some past information and then going to the present and into the future. If you see choices or options coming up for the person, give as many as possible, along with what steps the person would need to take to create the different scenarios available to him or her.

Notice your initial response to any questions your subject asks, as well as any information that comes to mind from the general reading.

After you've done this, put these perceptions to the side and answer the question as if for the first time.

Be as specific as possible and provide concrete descriptive information, especially with names and dates. Attempt to "translate" any information that comes through imagery or symbols into clear, conversational statements. If, for example, you get the image of a leafless tree in winter, you might conclude that this situation has run its course and needs time to find new steam.

When giving a reading for another, your intuitive impressions will often not make sense. Do not assume for this reason that this information is invalid. Especially when doing a reading on people close to us, our unconscious will often mask information to keep us from knowing things we don't want to or shouldn't know. You may also find that the other person relates to the words or images you use, even if they have no particular meaning for you.

Keep speaking continuously until you "feel complete" with the answer. When you have finished, the person may ask you additional questions or seek greater clarity about a point you made during the reading. If it does not interrupt your flow, the target can ask you questions during your reading. In most cases, however, the target should write these down and wait until the reading is over: all questions will usually be answered.

Sometimes your first sense will be changed by additional intuitive information. For example, your target may ask you: "What can I do to improve my relationship with Jim?" Your first sense may be that there is a lack of interest on Jim's part about the target person. As you intuit further, however, you may see that this is caused by Jim's feeling that her work difficulties are endless and she doesn't have time for a relationship right now. If your target really wants to deepen her relationship with Jim (and you will ask yourself intuitively if the course of action would produce a good relationship between the two of them), your intuition may suggest some ways to handle Jim's work as it affects your relationship.

Always Present Information Positively

Your goal during a reading is to give accurate, usable information. Telling someone that something definitely is or is not going to work doesn't usually accomplish this goal. Moreover, you might be wrong. It's best to simply describe the situation as you see it and as you intuit it progressing, without making judgments.

In giving the reading, then, pay special attention to your precise use of language. Express your impressions in a positive and empowering way. If you sense that the information as it is first revealed to you is too upsetting or unhelpful for your target, ask yourself questions. For example, I have had the occasion to sense a breakup in a relationship that my target thought was stable. Instead of giving this upsetting information as is, I ask myself questions:

- What will cause this breakup?
- Is there anything the target can do to prevent it?

If the dissolution appears to be a desirable thing (even if the individual doesn't realize this yet), I ask myself:

- What good things will result from the breakup?

After briefly asking myself these questions, I might say something like the following:

"I see the possibility of some distance coming up in your relationship. This distance is caused by a communication breakdown that resulted from an incident last December. I think that it's important to create some intimate occasions that facilitate communication, such as going to the theater together, or listening to music that you both enjoy. I feel that this distance, should it occur, will be a prelude to finding exactly the kind of connection that you have been looking for with someone else. I get the name 'Richard.'

"I feel the month of November. I also feel that you will be in a warm place at that time, maybe a vacation. Right now you should be working on making your day-to-day life more pleasurable, and on going out more with your own group of friends. I sense there is something that you have been thinking of working on in the last few months, an old talent perhaps, that you should start doing something about."

There are many situations that arise in reading a love relationship that have to be handled with great tact and delicacy. For example, I frequently see my targets trying to achieve impossible results from their relationships.

The best course of action is usually not to make your target feel more desperate about her relationship. Instead, look for constructive actions that will strengthen her sense of self. You should also focus on suggesting situations in her life in which the relationship might become less dominant. Finally, when I give a reading, I always begin by reminding the target that I can be wrong and that she should give the most weight to her own perceptions and insights, intuitive or otherwise.

How to Do Group Readings

Giving a group reading is not significantly different from giving a reading one-on-one. In a group reading, the person selected as the "target" sits in the center of the group with a pen and paper (and perhaps a tape recorder). The person writes down a specific question or issue about which she is looking for guidance. This may be a particular issue such as resolving a disagreement with her partner over where to spend the holidays, or a more general question like "What information will be helpful to me right now?"

When she is finished, she reads the question aloud to the group. The target should not, however, give background information, since this will only tempt the reader to use logic rather than intuition in answering the question.

All the readers do a body check. Then, as the intuitive information comes, they speak it freely to the person in the center. The readers should allow themselves to interrupt one another, or to follow someone else's lead with their own intuition. Remember that intuitive information includes interference. Someone else's intuitive information may trigger your own strong intuitive perceptions.

The body check should take less than a minute, and the reading of each person should take no longer than three to five minutes, depending on the size of the group. Remember that intuitive information appears in a flash, so it should not take long to convey it. If you have more information for the person, and you did not get a chance to express it, then write it down and give it to the person later.

After a few minutes, the person in the center may want to ask questions of the group. Focus on your own intuitions, even if other people in the group seem to be receiving contradictory impressions. You may be getting different sides of the same coin.

How Reliable Is Another Person's Reading?

We can learn to trust our own intuition, but we may still wonder how reliable someone else's reading for us is. One way to test the reader's intuitive accuracy is to start by asking a question that you know the answer to. But just because a reader provides an incorrect response to a question you already know the answer to does not mean that the whole reading is wrong. By and large, however, you should get the feeling that the person reading you is seeing clearly into your life, albeit from a different perspective.

Introducing the Envelope Technique

All members of your love support group may not be equally skilled at giving readings. Moreover, when a group has just begun meeting, members are often hesitant about revealing themselves too openly.

A useful technique in such situations—and one that you can even use for yourself—is to seal the target's question in an envelope. Doing so practically guarantees a purely intuitive reading, since the person giving it has no "clues" to work with (which any question inevitably provides).

The person giving the reading holds the envelope containing the question and reports her intuitive impressions as she would if she had actually heard the question read aloud. The target can then ask this person clarifying questions. When the reader's intuitive impressions come to a natural stop, she can open the envelope to further refine and interpret her insights.

Apart from being a fun group exercise, this technique can be adapted in many ways. For example, each participant can write her own question on a sheet, label the envelope in some identifying way (obviously not a name), and exchange envelopes. One by one, each person can give a reading without identifying the envelope she has. Someone should record these impressions for the person giving the reading (perhaps the person to her left), though everyone present will wonder whether the envelope is hers. After all the envelopes have been read, people can reveal their identifying symbols and claim their reading.

Love Support Groups on the Internet

Technology seems to be changing every aspect of modern life. This phenomenon is perhaps best epitomized by the Internet. Although many people are still a bit leery about revealing themselves online, the anonymity of the Internet, together with the way it allows far-flung people to interact, provide a unique forum for love support groups.

Concerns over privacy on the Internet are well founded, but with proper precautions you can avoid individuals with questionable motives and create a virtual group that meets regularly. There are a number of Web sites that allow people to create their own private chat rooms. As a starting point, check with your Internet service provider, such as America Online, or use popular search engines such as Yahoo or Infoseek.

Incidentally, one advantage of a Web-based group is that the participants need not reveal anything about themselves other than the screen name they use to identify themselves. Like the envelope technique, this forces everyone to be intuitive, since they have no information to go on. Another advantage to such groups is that people tend to be more honest when assured of the partial or complete anonymity of Web interactions.

Moving On to the Next Step

You should now be actively repatterning many aspects of your life with the support of your friends and your support network. We are now ready to consider what happens when you actually have love in your life (maybe you already do!). In addition to the personal issues that will arise, you'll need to work through the inevitable rough times between you and your partner. Even if you're not yet romantically involved, you can practice these techniques in the other important relationships in your life.

Checklist

- ❧ I create pleasure and the state of love in my life every day.
- ❧ I know how to receive intuitive information about myself and others, and how to project telepathically messages compatible with my love goal.
- ❧ I know what I want in a love relationship, and what I am willing to offer in return.
- ❧ I take active steps each day to affirm my goal.
- ❧ I have begun to clear space in my life for love.
- ❧ I am actively repatterning my inner life, especially by confronting hidden issues I may have about love relationships.
- ❧ I am actively repatterning my outer life, examining intuitively and otherwise the ways I present myself and interact with others.
- ❧ I reaffirm my friendships and other meaningful relationships, and I continually practice my relationship skills.
- ❧ I have begun to develop a support network to help me on my love journey.

STEP FIVE

Caring for Your Garden
(Thorns and All)

Love Byte

Coping with the Challenges
of a Relationship

*If you have followed the previous steps, then you are now in a
beginning relationship—if only dating—or perhaps you were already
seriously involved with someone when you began reading this book.
Like any friendship, a romantic relationship has its ups and downs.
We now turn our attention to working through the difficulties and
challenges you may face.*

*The difficulties you experience in your relationship may be caused
by external pressures such as a major change in one partner's job.
These pressures are not necessarily bad—a job promotion, for example—but they must be negotiated carefully by both of you.*

*Even if you are not involved with someone romantically, it is
important to know how to work out difficulties with your friends. This
step, then, gives you some tools about how to work things through.*

*One powerful tool is a "telepathic dialogue." A telepathic dialogue
allows you to communicate with someone else and to send that person
a message, without actually confronting him. This allows you to
anticipate how the person will respond when you actually do speak
face-to-face, and to get a better sense both of his needs and of how
best to communicate your needs.*

Even if you are not currently involved with someone romantically, you can use the telepathic dialogue technique to work out difficulties with your friends—or even with your future partner. Of course, using this technique doesn't do away with the need for face-to-face conversations.

○ 11 ○

Making It Work:
Putting Your Relationship Skills
to Work

Negotiating the Rough Spots

In the last step, we discussed the importance of friendships and your other important relationships both to help you repattern your life and to develop and practice your relationship skills. Like any friendship, a romantic relationship will inevitably have its share of difficult moments. So let's turn our attention now to working through these difficulties and challenges.

The Four Fundamental Challenges of
All Romantic Relationships

Romantic relationships are incredibly rewarding on so many levels, but they also present us with challenges that must be carefully negotiated by both partners. Some of these challenges are external, arising outside the relationship itself, and are nobody's "fault." Such challenges include a major change in either partner's career. Or—knock on wood—a serious illness. Or even the joyous birth of a child.

Note, by the way, that challenges are not necessarily problems. Nonetheless, they produce demands on one or both of you that can affect the relationship.

I believe that any of these external challenges can be successfully met if both partners can successfully meet the *internal* ones. As I see it, the four primary challenges of any relationship are the following:

- **Being able to communicate not only your thoughts and feelings to your partner, but also your needs and expectations.** Communication involves not just saying things clearly but also saying them in a way that our partner both understands and *wants* to respond to. For example, if you feel that your partner is not listening to your needs, you must communicate with him in a way that makes him *want* to listen. This means you must be willing to express your needs, which is not always easy. ("You don't understand me" often means "You are not satisfying my needs or expectations.")

- **Being able, in turn, to listen and understand your partner's needs.** This involves listening skills, which we discussed in the previous chapter. It also involves your being discerning, since your partner may not be able to express his needs clearly, both major ones and day-to-day ones. (You may recall that we used I-mode to embody and get in touch with the needs of others.)

- **Being able to resolve disputes, misunderstandings, and disappointments.** This goes beyond mere "he said–she said" communication skills. It includes a willingness to recognize and confront these things as well as a willingness to compromise. This, like the other challenges, requires us to be sensitive to our partner's moods. It also requires us, as we discussed in Step Two, to strive to maintain the integrity of a relationship, and for both parties to be sensitive to their own unmet needs as well as those of their partner.

- **Being able to accept your "couple self" without denying or losing touch with your "individual self."** Each partner must find the common ground in the relationship while accepting the separate ground. This is commonly referred to as "maintaining boundaries." One way to ensure this is to focus on pleasure. When we give up the interests or activities that made us who we were before the relationship (sometimes doing it "for" the other person), we create a potential double whammy for our partner. First, we grow to resent the sacrifice we made ("And to think I did it for you!") and second, we aren't ourselves, the person our partner fell in love with in the first place! Another way not to lose your individual self within a romantic relationship is to maintain your friendships, as we discussed in the previous chapter. "Maintaining boundaries" is so important that we will explore it throughout the sixth and final step in our love journey.

These are not the only challenges a relationship faces, of course, but they are the most critical ones. The exercises and techniques in this chapter will strengthen your relationship skills to help build your relationship and to ensure that it endures.

The Vital Importance of Honest Communication: Ask and Listen

People often forget how important the direct communication of needs and ideas is. If you want a friend or lover to respond to you differently, you can use the various exercises in this book to work through the problem on an intuitive level. This does not replace the importance of speaking with the person about your feelings and the need for change.

I have a very good friend who used to have a bad habit of phrasing her advice in a hard-edged, sharply critical way. I found her tone was so consistently hurtful that I finally decided to confront her directly. When I did, I emphasized the positive aspects of our relationship and requested that she be more aware of her tone when speaking with me during my more vulnerable moments. As a result, she now knew exactly how to respond in my times of need. The change was not burdensome for her. On the contrary, it was actually beneficial in allowing this very loving person to present her help in a gentler way. This also resulted in her being perceived as kinder by her other friends.

For further ideas on this topic, you may want to return to our earlier discussion of how to present information positively during a reading (page 171).

Communication 101

There are countless popular books and articles on the communication that goes on—or doesn't go on—between men and women. Most of these academic experts (often sociologists or anthropologists) speculate on how the gender differences in conversation contribute to misunderstandings between the sexes.

Yet they all approach communication in an idealized way. They assume that the person speaking has a clear message that is somehow garbled or misinterpreted by the listener. We never see an analysis by the experts of real-world communication, in which there are no clear messages, and nobody ever says exactly what he or she means, and most people don't even know what they mean in the first place.

I'm reminded of Alice in Wonderland, who complained, "I never know what I'm thinking until I say it!" How often that is true for us, too. Maybe it's that we know what we're feeling—say, angry—but we don't know why. Unfortunately, this kind of thinking out loud can easily trigger an emotional response in the listener, which can escalate into a heated argument. How many times have you regretted something you said to your partner about a sensitive matter? Or maybe you know what you want to say and even how to say it, but you don't know how the other person will respond. Or maybe the other person isn't there. Or maybe you haven't even met the person!

It may surprise you that you can carry on a conversation in each of these situations using telepathy. I'll show you how shortly.

The Three Levels of Communication

Relationships take place on three levels: the conscious, the unconscious, and the intuitive. The conscious level is the one we generally interact on. We are aware, say, that though our partner is funny and we are serious, we share similar goals. We admire each other and feel that we can create a good life together despite our differences. We work hard at our relationship and we make it a priority.

The unconscious level includes the patterning of our individual histories and how they play out in our relationships. It also includes qualities that we "project" onto our partner (he's strong, he's reliable) that may or may not truly be part of his character. Although we are not aware of this level, it influences all our perceptions and actions.

The intuitive level of communication is, in a sense, the most intimate, although again we are not generally aware of its influence or even existence. This level consists of the continual dialogue of thought, feeling, and imagery that goes back and forth between you and your partner. It's knowing what your partner needs—or resents—without being told. It's knowing what your partner is doing and why. It is knowing every cell of who your partner *truly* is—as opposed to his "public" face, or even the face he presents to himself—and who he is trying to become.

Miscommunication Is Often Based on Different Perceptions

You say tuh-MAY-toe and I say tuh-MAH-toe. Maybe we should just agree to call it a red fruit that grows on the vine and tastes good with olive oil and salt. What, you don't like salt?

Each person has different tastes, different values, different histories, and a different way of viewing things.

The same smile can be viewed as friendly by one person and seductive by another. A masterful air could be felt as gallant by one woman and chauvinistic by another. (I'll never forget when my brother as a boy held a door open for a women in a store and the woman railed against him for his "chauvinistic" ways.)

I recall one student who felt that her lover had lost interest in her sexually. She assumed that it was because in the past few months she had put on weight. The idea that his love for her could be so shallow hurt her deeply. When she did the exercise, however, she became aware that he felt she had shown a lack of interest in his work-related projects. He interpreted this as her having lost respect for him and his ideas. She experimented with changing her behavior, and it paid off. They were headed for estrangement because they had both misinterpreted the language of the other.

If we are to communicate well, we must understand where the other person is coming from. The following exercise will help you understand how your lover's (or friend's) perceptions differ from your own, and how you can best express your love as well as your needs and concerns.

EXERCISE 26: RE-CREATING EXPERIENCES

Allow yourself to remember the last conversation you had with a romantic interest that did not go as well as you would have liked. Use all of your senses to re-create a moment—any moment—in that interaction. Continue to do this until you can sense the interaction as if it were taking place right now.

Now allow yourself to become the other person. Use all your senses: feeling what he was feeling, seeing what he was seeing, thinking what he was thinking, and so on. Allow yourself to notice how he perceived you and the interaction.

Record your impressions.

One Person's Example

I sense that he wants to feel more in control in the relationship because he is feeling tired, angry, and overwhelmed. He is expressing his anger without taking responsibility for it. He does this by withdrawing some of the feeling and responses he knows I need and expect from him. My normal tendency would be to shut down and not communicate, but that would be neither healthy for our relationship nor enlightening for me.

He does not want to lose the relationship, but neither does he want to be devoured by it. He needs to feel that I am solidly in my own life: to witness my going out with my own friends or to have interests not connected to him.

It's important to change the current dynamic before he feels overwhelmed by his anger. He is almost daring me to leave. When I move toward him in what he experiences as an aggressive way (which for me is open and loving), he shuts down. I see myself being consistently caring in little ways, like stroking his head or remembering something he likes and getting it for him. I need to let go of the idea and the feeling that our relationship has to change or become something else. I have to find a way to simply allow it to be.

I need to be clear about what I want and need for myself and to let him know at a future time. I always want to discuss things the moment I am feeling them, and often I sense that these are the times he is the least receptive. I need to go back to my love goal and put my focus back on myself and not on our relationship, while still allowing some gentle attention to be on him. He will relax as I do this, and the positive energy will return to our relationship in a month or so.

Discussion

As the old saying goes, what is sauce for the goose is not always sauce for the gander. By focusing your attention and intuition on how the other person perceives the words, needs, and expectations you are sending, you can help create more effective communication and interaction.

Intuition Offers Perspective—and Choices

Many misunderstandings in relationships arise because we overpersonalize another's words or actions. In doing so, we let them take on a significance they don't necessarily have. By providing additional information, intuition broadens our limited perspective. It not only gives us information about the present and future, but also allows us to revisit and reevaluate experiences from the past.

Imagine that your high school sweetheart decided to leave your hometown and attend college far away. Lacking a detached intuitive perspective, you might have felt unimportant and abandoned at the time, and later carried this fear over into your subsequent relationships.

Intuition gives us a broader, more objective picture of circumstances and motivations. By using your intuition in the situation above, you might have realized that it was your boyfriend's home life, and not you, that he felt compelled to escape.

This new information gives you choices. If you were still a teenager you could respond from a position of sympathy and support for your boyfriend's needs, rather than one of hurt and resentment. If you were an adult looking back on your past with this new insight, you could recognize the cause of your fear of abandonment and not allow it to interfere with your current relationships. We draw conclusions based on our interpretation of past events that our unconscious stores as fact. Intuition can help you reevaluate some of those facts and rewrite the rules you live by.

A Broader Perspective Can Be Challenging

Surprisingly, intuition's ability to give us access to another's perspective can actually work against us. For example, intuition can allow us to so identify with our partner's point of view that we give up our own needs or identity. Or we can intuitively pick up another's interest in us and confuse his passion for our own. And since intuition can see into the future, it's easy to confuse future possibilities with current realities.

If you knew every selfish or mean-spirited thing about your partner, you'd probably leave him. If you knew about every time your partner did the wrong thing, you'd lose respect for him. If you knew about every time your partner had been wronged, you'd be flooded by compassion. If you knew every honorable thing about your partner, you'd probably treasure him more than air itself.

The challenge intuition presents us with is to hold these conflicting levels of awareness within our realm of perception. We will then be able to develop an esteem and caring for our partner—and for ourselves—that is genuine, perceptive, and *unique*. The power of caring from the intuitive perspective, and being cared for, is immense because its loving is not blind but rather powerfully, profoundly *knowing*. It cannot be replaced by another, for it exists only between you and your partner.

The only way to do that thoroughly is through intuition. Intuition allows you to see through the eyes and experiences of others, and thus to see yourself as they see you. The ability to perceive another's experiences and values firsthand allows you to make contact with that person in a profound way. Intuition will allow you to perceive another in the most personal and intimate way either of you has ever experienced.

How Your Intuition Can Mislead You

It may seem strange that I would be admitting that intuition can interfere with our conscious goals. Remember that what I'm referring to here is unconsciously directed, untrained intuition. Please keep in mind that your intuition is operating all the time to supply you with information, whether or not you realize it. The tricky thing is that until you gain some awareness of how to direct your intuition, it often isn't clear where information is coming from or what it is addressing. This can lead to confusion when intuitive information flies in the face of what your logic is telling you.

Let's take a simple example. You're looking forward to an office picnic this weekend. Your intuition, however, has sensed that it is going to rain that day, so it tries to get you to make alternate plans. If you're not consciously listening to your intuition, you'll feel conflicted as your conscious intellect tries to justify why you shouldn't go to the picnic. The result is a feeling of anxiety without knowing the cause. This is why it's important to listen to our intuition when it nudges us.

Let's look at an example closer to home, this one involving a budding relationship. You've just met someone that you like. Your intuition, however, has just picked up on the fact that the guy—let's not be delicate—is a slob. You, on the other hand, are an inveterate neatnik. Your intuition might lead you to repel this person, a decision that your conscious mind would then have to rationalize. This could be unfortunate, since his sloppiness is something you might have been able to work through. This might have been possible had you been aware that his sloppiness was the real reason you just lost interest.

Untrained intuition can also interfere with existing relationships. Let's say you spend an afternoon trying to ignore your feelings of resentment or anger by acting sweet with your partner. While not consciously aware of your underlying negativity, your partner may detect it intuitively. Sensing your anger, he may react to your apparent kindness not lovingly, but with irritation or defensiveness. You might then in turn react with hurt or anger. Somewhere in this process communication is destroyed and confusion is born.

By becoming aware of your intuition, you gain choices. If you know you're angry, you can simply state it and address the task of clearing the issue up. If you don't realize you're angry, you only notice the other person's response to your behavior. But instead of reacting to that response emotionally, you could take some intuitive distance and use one of the many exercises in this book to give you a read on what is really going on. You can then address it directly.

For example, instead of acting nice (when you don't really want to), you can give your partner an intuitive gift by acting with passion (the centers for passion and anger are located in the same place in the brain). Another approach would be to shift perspectives and ask yourself the intuitive question "How can I approach my partner right now to give him something he needs, and also get something I need?" You can do this, even if you don't consciously know what that thing is or what either of you is feeling.

If the positions are reversed and you sense something amiss in the attitude of your partner, intuition once again gives you choices about how to approach the situation. For example, you could get some intuitive information about what is going on inside him so that you don't take his responses personally. You could look for some information about how best to approach him, which words or gestures he would be able to respond to most positively. If you didn't feel you could cope with the situation directly and wanted to give him a chance to cool down, you could stay late at work and avoid the potential conflict entirely.

Unacknowledged Expectations Can Cause Great Disappointments

Our personal feelings of disappointment are often a result of seeking validation from our partner. The need for validation puts both parties in a no-win situation. This is because nobody can successfully reassure us about something that we feel in our hearts to be untrue. If we do not believe in ourselves, the reassurances of others—even loved ones— are not likely to convince us. We're disappointed, but it is because we expect our partner to do something we must do for ourselves.

Most disappointments are caused because something happened that we did not expect, or because we expected something that didn't happen. Someone once said that the art of relationships is the art of managing expectations. This is certainly true. The tricky thing about expectations is that many of them are unspoken. For example, we expect our partner to bring us something special at least once a week. It doesn't have to be big or expensive—just a little reminder of his affection. The problem is that we never *tell* them that is what we expect. Usually lurking somewhere in the background of these expectations is the phrase "If he really loved me, he would bring me flowers every day," or "If he really loved me, he would communicate with me more often," or whatever.

Another problem with expectations is that we're not always aware of them—even of our own. (You might want to refer to our earlier discussion of how you experience love.) This is especially true in love relationships, since each person has a romantic fantasy that forms at a very young age. If you want to understand how your partner has disappointed you in the past (or may in the future), you need to get in touch with your expectations. Naturally, this also applies to your partner: you need a way to discover his expectations, including his unspoken and unconscious ones.

How Do You Know You're Loved?

Perhaps the greatest disappointment we experience in a relationship is not feeling loved. Each person experiences love differently. It's important to note that sometimes we are loved, although we—or the person who loves us—may not be able to put those feelings into words but rather express it through actions and gestures. *So how do you know when you feel loved?*

We rarely ask ourselves this question consciously, and as a result we often are not aware of our mounting disappointment until it is too late to salvage the relationship. The next exercise will help you become more aware of your romantic expectations.

EXERCISE 27: HE LOVES ME, HE LOVES ME NOT

Take a moment to look back on the times in your life when you've felt loved and the times when you've felt in love, and write a paragraph about each.

Now look at what you've written and give some detailed actions or gestures that would let you know that you are loved or in love. You may find that some of the things seem to defy explanation. Try anyway. Anything you have trouble describing is something you are unlikely to obtain or recognize that you've obtained even if you have it.

For example, maybe you feel loved when you feel totally accepted. Unless you can define in concrete terms what words, actions, attitudes, or gestures helped you feel that way, it will be hard for you to know when you're receiving that kind of acknowledgment. Without this concrete understanding, you will keep fulfilling love only in the realm of fantasy, where it's likely to stay. There will always be an element of love that defies definition, but you should be able to identify which basic cues tell you that you are in love.

Completing the following statements will reveal a great deal about what you value and expect in a love relationship:

- A person who loves someone else will always:
- A person who loves someone else will never:
- A person knows she is in love when she:
- I know he loves me because:
- I know he doesn't love me because:

Example No. 1

I feel loved when I feel essential to the other person's well-being. When they need me in body, mind, and spirit. I need someone to recognize the best in me, and to think beyond his own needs and desires to want to care for me. I feel loved when someone strives to show me the world from his eyes and heart.

I feel in love when my life with the other person is better than it is without him. I need to feel tenderness when I look at him. I need to feel that in some way he surpasses me in looks, intelligence, and morality. I need to feel a certain physical need for him, not all of the time but at least in intimate moments. I need to be able to see what we are building.

Example No. 2

I noticed that in my memories of feeling in love, I was enchanted with the way the person I loved interacted with the world. I wanted to take his hand and follow him into new experiences. I fall in love with the way people express their ideas, and I know I'm in love when I want to listen to them and know more about all of their thoughts and perceptions. I know I'm in love when I feel that it is a privilege to take care of a person. I must have the sense that the person is essentially good and honorable, so that I feel good about caring. I feel in love when I am able to have a common vision of the future with someone. When I am in love, I feel a strong desire to be physically intimate with the person, and even the thought of him evokes a powerful physical sensation of desire.

Example No. 3

I have felt loved in the past when my partner expressed sexual desire toward me and let me know what he found desirable about me as an individual. I have felt loved when I have awakened to find my partner looking at me or stroking my hair. I have felt loved when I have heard, secondhand, that my partner has defended me in conversation, or when my partner seeks my opinion on little things (the big things I take for granted). I have felt loved when my partner notices little things, like that I'm running low on matching socks or that I'm eating too much salt.

Discussion

People love and show love in different ways. If you're in a relationship, it's very helpful to see your partner's detailed lists. You can use your telepathy and your empathy to understand why these qualities represent love for him, and then adopt some of them as your own.

If you are not in a relationship, this exercise serves a dual purpose. First, it helps you to understand more clearly what you are looking for. Second, it allows you to identify the people in your environment who make you feel loved, and why. Third, it can help you learn how you can express love to yourself.

When I wasn't in a relationship, I took to buying myself flowers every week. I realized that going without this simple pleasure just because someone else was not doing it for me was depriving myself unnecessarily.

I had a long talk with my mate about how he knows he is loved and conversely, what I do that makes him feel unloved. He made a very interesting observation. When a potential buyer points out an objection to a salesperson, it's because he's already leaning strongly toward a purchase, or he wouldn't bother voicing the objection. He feels loved when I battle to improve an aspect of his behavior that isn't working for me. He feels unloved when I criticize him. Oddly enough, I pointed out (critical to the end) that the same behavior makes him feel both loved and unloved.

Using Intuition to Work Through Disappointments

Every relationship has its moments of disappointment. If you don't acknowledge these disappointments, they get caught up in your feelings about yourself or your partner and strangle the relationship. His socks on the bathroom floor become a statement about how much he values you, which then attaches itself to the feeling that your mother didn't give you the respect you deserved as a child, which attaches to something else, and so on. By the time he comes home with a huge bunch of fresh flowers to let you know how much he loves you—"I spent an hour after work picking them in the park for you"—you're so angry and resentful that you wonder why he didn't get something less ostentatious.

Everyone has witnessed, if not been a partner in, a relationship that started with great promise, only to end bitterly as different disappointments piled up. Disappointments that we do not confront and resolve can erode any relationship.

Yet disappointment and disillusionment can actually provide the impetus for growth and change in any healthy union. By recognizing our disappointed expectations and coming to terms with some while shedding others (the unrealistic ones), we accommodate new growth both in ourselves and in the relationship.

While the best time to notice and talk about both achievements and disappointments is when they arise, it's not always possible to do so in a nurturing way. Perhaps the disappointment has become such a charged issue that there is no way to speak about it calmly. Perhaps you have argued about it so many times that you each have become unwilling even to consider a change in behavior or point of view.

The following exercise will help guide you in working through disappointments, both in yourself and in others. Read through these instructions for this exercise before beginning. Don't worry about remembering them. Simply read them through once and then begin.

EXERCISE 28: GETTING BEYOND PAST DISAPPOINTMENTS

You can sit down or lie back for this exercise, keeping a pad and pencil in one hand. I recommend that you keep your eyes closed, opening them only when you need to jot down a key word to help you recall your information.

Now allow your unconscious to give you information about

your feelings of disappointment. Be especially aware of the memories your unconscious provides you, even if they don't make sense to you right now.

When you've completed this, do a body check. Now allow your intuition to provide you with information about how to heal these disappointments. Again, don't worry about how your intuitive impressions will help you do this. Simply trust that they will, and jot down whatever information your intuition provides. You can make sense of it after the exercise.

During this exercise, you may have become aware of relationships that need healing. If so, simply allow your intuition to respond to the question "What action or telepathic intention do I need right now to heal the relationship?" While not the primary goal of this exercise, this part will frequently allow you to experience the other person's state directly. So long as you keep your awareness on the target question, you can allow this to happen.

One Person's Example

The memory is of us getting ready to go to bed. Roger says "good night, I love you" in an offhand way, and turns off the light. He used to move close to me, yet for some reason tonight I notice that I have been feeling alone.

I'm getting the memory of ninth grade. My best friend has made friends with another girl, and they are leaving me out of secrets. I am hurt and angry. I trusted her more than that.

Intuitively I get the feeling that Roger needs more rest. He has been working hard, and I have been so grumpy lately that he doesn't feel that he can come to me for comfort. To heal the wound, I need to feel that he is working on feeling and expressing his love to me. I need to let him know that his attitude is making me feel alone. I get a picture of us in bed, touching toes. I am reading a book and he is tapping away on his laptop, but we are together and close. He has had some recent back surgery, so I need to get a pillow to help him do this comfortably. I feel connected, and he is getting some of his pile of work done.

Intuitively I am letting my ninth-grade friend see my tears and not caring if she teases me. I am not holding my feelings in so she can conveniently ignore my presence.

I sent an impression of myself crying as a child to my childhood friend, and as I did, I realized that she probably didn't realize that I was hurt. I get a sense of her not understanding why I didn't join them in their plans. I am beginning to realize how I tend to close down and then perceive it as rejection by others.

I send a telepathic message to Roger with the feeling of my hurt and loneliness, and an image of what would make it better. I need him to gather me up in his arms every once in a while with the same intensity he had before I was always available to him. He needs to make this gesture because I feel that if I ask for it directly and he does it I won't know or feel like it is really coming from his own desire. I hope he gets this message.

Discussion

You will notice that at the beginning of the exercise we are allowing unconscious and intuitive information to make itself available to us. This information—which might be a memory of how you experienced a situation, or how you think you experienced a situation, or how you remember an experience, even if your recollection is not technically correct—influences all of your actions.

Our subconscious does not make subtle distinctions between whether an event or one's recollection of it are the same, and the memory gets filed away, affecting our future behavior. If you think your lover has been unkind to you, for example, you remember his unkindness—regardless of whether or not he actually was rude. Naturally it's important to understand as much as we can about the information—real or imagined, true or false—on which we base our thoughts, feelings, and actions.

When you have a sense of what your partner needs to hear or experience in order to heal the rift between you, you can apply these insights when communicating with him.

Transforming Difficulties and Anger into Passion

Unresolved disappointments usually lead to anger, which in turn leads to conflict. Conflict provides us with tension, and tension creates energy. If this tension and energy are channeled properly, they can provide the fuel to transform your relationship and yourself. If this tension and energy become blocked, however, it can be destructive.

I'm sure you've had the experience of being involved in an argument with your partner that you thought would spell the end of the relationship, yet which ultimately led to a deepened connection between the two of you. Without the pull of gravity, we would fall from the earth. Tension is a necessary and unavoidable element in all things in the physical world, including our relationships.

But the exact moment when you feel tension in a relationship—whether that tension is positive or negative—is the exact moment when it's the most difficult not to overreact. This is also the moment when it's most important to *act,* not react, with consideration. Reacting often causes you to introduce old unconscious cycles into the relationship. Your scenarios are then met with one of your lover's own unconscious cycles. This sets in motion the recurring "resolving-past-conflicts-by-tormenting-your-lover-with-what-Daddy-or-Mommy-didn't-do-right" game.

Let's say, for example, that your lover has not been attentive lately. You were the youngest child in your family, and you felt that everyone had either done everything first or everything better by the time you came along. Your solution was always to do something so outrageous that it had to be noticed. In this reactive mode, rooted in past experiences, you acted totally inappropriately at a party you went to with your lover.

Now let's say that as the only son in the family, he was expected to watch over the girls, a job he deeply resented. One of the things he originally loved about you was the way you seemed to know yourself and the world, and to be grounded in it. When you act totally out of character at the party, he starts reacting the way he did with his sisters—and resenting it just as much. You get the attention you need, but it also entangles both of you in a scripted drama that would be better resolved than acted out.

If you are alone, or feeling alone in a relationship, it is very likely that you are trapped in such a scripted drama. If so, remember that you have options. The relationship you want now is active and responsive, not reactive.

The following exercise introduces a technique that takes only a few moments to use. With practice, it can be employed whenever you get that uncomfortable but compelling feeling that you need to react.

EXERCISE 29: STEPPING BACK TO REFLECT

When you feel tension in your relationship, ask yourself the following questions:

- What does my partner need to perceive right now in order to change this dynamic into a positive or bonding one?

- Is there any "catalyst" I could introduce to improve the dynamic of our relationship? *For example, taking a walk with your partner every evening after dinner to improve communication, or getting your lover a glass of water in the middle of an argument.*

- What is my inner tension urging me to resolve?

These questions are only guides. As you become more accustomed to using your intuition, it will provide you with questions and responses that directly address your target.

One Person's Example

I was in a slow death situation in my relationship. I was experiencing tension as a result of her seeming less in love. I responded by feeling let down and angry. When I looked at the tension, my intuition inundated me with unexpected information. I instinctively perceived her tension as the feeling that I no longer truly wanted the dreams we had started the relationship with. I realized that my tension stemmed from putting all the burden of feeling pleasure in my life on the relationship. The catalyst was to begin to do out-of-the-ordinary things to give both of us more pleasure, and not to expect her to provide it.

I did a really nice thing. I got off work a few hours early and I bought flowers, dinner, and a video we'd both wanted to see. Then I warned her not to bring home any work because I had some projects around the house that we needed to do together. I felt intuitively that if I told her that I had a surprise, she would feel pressured to be loving and intimate, even if that was not where she was at the moment. That's also why I rented the video. I felt that I needed to send the message that I wanted to be with her without having to take pleasure from her.

The evening ended with both of us crying because it melted a lot of pain we had each been feeling. We talked about the fact that when she feels I am angry she withdraws because she feels judged. I expressed my need for her to be able to speak with me at those times, because her withdrawal just makes me angrier.

Discussion

Even in the healthiest of relationships, some of the dynamics are bound to get stuck or frozen from time to time. Often a small shift in perspective or behavior can make a huge change in the relationship, and open the door for communication, forgiveness, and intimacy. If too many problems are left untended, the structure of a relationship cannot bear the weight and will eventually collapse. Difficulties become opportunities for strengthening a relationship—when they are worked through. In a bone that has been broken, the site of the break actually heals back *stronger*. This can be true of the anatomy of relationships as well.

The Telepathic Dialogue Technique

Have you ever wanted to say something important to someone—ask *him* out on a date, ask your boss for a raise, complain to a neighbor— but hesitated because you didn't know how the other person would respond? We all have.

And in such situations we often rehearse what we're going to say before we pick up the phone, like an actor practicing her lines. Sometimes we even close our eyes to imagine how the other person will respond.

Telepathic dialogues are similar. The difference between a telepathic dialogue and an imagined conversation is that you are actually sending the message, not just rehearsing it. Another difference is that in the telepathic dialogue you are embodying both parts of the dialogue equally, playing both yourself and your partner in a given situation.

In a sense, this technique combines telepathy and I-mode. You may recall from our earlier discussion that telepathy is the sending and receiving of thoughts and feelings, while I-mode allows us to fully embody the thoughts and feelings of another, almost becoming this person. A telepathic dialogue allows you to communicate with someone and to send him a message, without actually confronting the person. Telepathic dialogues also allow you to hear the other side (which is especially helpful when your partner is uncommunicative), anticipating how the person will respond when you actually do speak face-to-face. In doing so, you will get a better sense of his needs and how best to communicate your own.

You can even use this technique on yourself to discover what you're really feeling. Telepathic dialogue helps you reach your unconscious and communicate with the different parts of your personality. It can also broaden your ability to communicate and resolve problems with those you would like to be closer to. You can create a starting point of internal understanding that will create success in your relationships.

Even before you have a romantic interest in someone specific, you can use the telepathic dialogue technique to work out difficulties with your friends—or even with your future partner. Throughout this book, you have been practicing how to deepen and shift your awareness. In an earlier exercise, for example, you used I-mode to put your focus on your partner (or another person) and to embody his needs and perceptions—in a sense to stand in his shoes.

Remember that a telepathic dialogue requires you to focus not only on yourself but also on your partner and the interaction between you. Although you can do a telepathic dialogue without taking notes, I suggest that you use a tape recorder so that you can clearly recall what was resolved, and how it was resolved, as a guide for future interactions.

Four Examples of Telepathic Dialogues

You can use the telepathic dialogue in many situations, with people you know, with people you have yet to meet, and even with yourself (perhaps its most powerful application). The following examples will illustrate a variety of situations:

- A husband using it to communicate with his wife
- A man using it after a bad breakup with his lover
- A woman using it with a man she has never met
- A woman using it to communicate with her hidden or subconscious self

Example No. 1

I need you to be more supportive, so that something is waiting for me after my long days at work. I feel her responding that "everybody needs me: my children, my friends, you." I sense her being unable to hold up under the additional weight of my demands.

She wonders what happened to the two adults who used to enjoy a glass of wine and speak with each other about art and ideas and life and the world. I don't know how to respond immediately, but I am overcome with the feeling that I have forgotten to relate to her as anything but my wife and the mother of our children.

I send to her a desire to take some time tonight to sit down together and have a conversation. I send her a message about our having a housekeeper. I let her know how much better our life would be if she would allow somebody else to do some of the chores that she doesn't have time to do.

I sense her feeling hurt, as if I'm saying that she is not doing a good enough job, and I quickly send to her that having time to be together is the most important thing for both of us. I feel some compromise, and I will continue to send that to her telepathically. I will also make a point of saying that to her when I get home tonight.

Example No. 2

In my body check, I feel tired deeply. The back of my neck hurts. I'm feeling a little spacey. I notice the darkness of the apartment. I also notice my pleasure in the contacts I've had today with old friends. My head itches. Scratching brings immediate relief. I wish all solutions to problems could be that simple.

As I begin my intuitive dialogue, I sense Jane's being very downcast, perhaps even brokenhearted, although her anger has subsided. She doesn't really know what to do anymore or who to turn to for advice or comfort. Her health is not very good; she may even be crying a lot these days. The disappointments are all mixed together for her, so much so that I need to ask myself intuitively which one to address first. "Why did you leave me?" is what I hear. "I did everything for you and it wasn't enough," she continues.

I ask my intuitive self how I can respond so that she can hear me and we can heal the relationship. I send back to her with all of the senses the following message: "Look at me. I'm still here. You don't have to search to find me. My heart is still with you, but that isn't really what you want."

I sense her reply: "I wanted something other than what you were giving me, some basic human kindnesses and honesty and friendship. Those are things that I still want from you now. I don't think either of us knows how to extricate ourselves from the bind in which we have trapped ourselves. Hurting me is not going to get you anything." I get the sense of her wanting me to know that she doesn't love me and doesn't need me. But I have not forgotten the dreams we shared, and I am heartbroken.

I get the sense, however, that she doesn't truly believe she doesn't need me. If she did believe it, the thought would simply fan her desire to hurt me. I sit and wait for intuition to give me a guide. I see myself standing strong. If she wants to come toward me I will be here for her, and I send that telepathically to her. I can feel that there is no resolution right now.

I ask myself what she needs from me in this dialogue to get things moving on the right track. I hear the words "go in peace," like at the end of a church service, and I send this message from my heart to hers. I feel the pain in both of our hearts, and I realize that this is the message that I have to send every time I think of her or our relationship: "go in peace."

I get the sense that she doesn't feel that she can leave the anger without leaving an important part of herself behind. I see her taking or having what she needs, and realizing it. Once again I send her the message "go in peace." Now I get a strong impression of her needing to know that I will still be here if she lets go. I feel able to send that feeling to her. In doing so, I feel that I open the door for friendship.

Example No. 3

I see the sea and the mountains with this person living in between them. There is space in his house, but no one to fill it. He has experienced a great deal of motion in his life without much emotion. He is waiting to anchor the emotion in partnership with a mate before he expresses it. I decide to be receptive first, but I don't feel him calling me because he feels no reason to call out anymore. He is not depressed about this; instead he accepts the possibility that love may not be for him.

He is in his late forties. I send a message to him that I'm coming. I also send the message that I need the space he has left for me, but that I wish it were filled with some hope or expectation that I would arrive. (The month of June just popped into my head as my arrival time.) I want a guide back out into life. I have energy and liveliness to add to his life and his space.

I still feel him incapable of movement, and I feel myself singing to him. I see paintings and his having something to do with these paintings. I feel him moved by the sound and drawn to the source. I think he will recognize me right away. It may take me longer to recognize him.

I hear him say that he is willing to fight my dragons for me. He wants to show me that he can win and I can rest. I don't know how I feel about this. He responds that he is not speaking of promises, but of slain dragons placed at my feet as I build for him a home in the woods.

Example No. 4

I notice my attention going to my heart and to my head. My head is angry, angry with my heart and angry in general. My heart is shying away from my head and wanting to protect its tenderness. I tell my heart to stand up for itself, that my head cannot hear it anymore. My heart's response that here is no place for it to stand up. It is as if the ceiling is too low.

I look for another solution. I see my heart begin to breathe, to pump so loudly I can hear it in my head. I ask my head if it can get out of the way a little. Meditation may work. I let my heart expand because I am feeling empty without it. My head responds that it is ready to get out of the way as long as my heart will protect me as well as my head has. My heart responds that it doesn't know how. My head suggests that it should stay inside its own body to provide strength instead of always hopping outside into other people's lives, into hope or into the unknown.

I see myself as a young child performing in front of a mirror, desperately wanting an audience but being too self-conscious to act when I actually had one. I ask myself why this might be. I get the same picture of my head and my heart. I get the feeling that I was so unaccustomed to receiving any attention as a child that when someone actually paid attention to me, the strangeness of it made me want to run. I am sending the message to myself to stay in my heart and to allow myself to be seen without worrying about who is seeing me. I accept this message.

Discussion

During a telepathic dialogue, if both you and your partner are sending and receiving messages, you will need to allow your senses both to send and receive information, as your reasoning mind notices the change in both your partner and yourself.

Bear in mind that telepathy is not mind control. You cannot and should not try to bend someone to your point of view. Telepathy is simply the ability to convey a message to another person intuitively in a way that allows him to understand and accept it. Using a telepathic dialogue is as likely to change your attitude and response as it is your partner's. Because its primary purpose is to work through difficulties and misunderstandings, it inevitably leads to compromise on both sides.

Moving On to Our Sixth and Final Step

We've almost reached the end of our journey. Whether or not you already have the love you want in your life, you have developed all the tools you need. In the next step you will celebrate what you've achieved.

Checklist

- ⅏ I create pleasure and the state of love in my life every day.
- ⅏ I know how to receive intuitive information about myself and others, and how to project telepathically messages compatible with my love goal.
- ⅏ I know what I want in a love relationship, and what I am willing to offer in return.
- ⅏ I take active steps each day to affirm my goal.
- ⅏ I have begun to clear space in my life for love.
- ⅏ I am actively repatterning my inner life, especially by confronting hidden issues I may have about love relationships.

⟋ I am actively repatterning my outer life, examining intuitively and otherwise the ways I present myself and interact with others.

⟋ I reaffirm my friendships and other meaningful relationships, and I continually practice my relationship skills.

⟋ I have begun to develop a support network to help me on
my love journey.

STEP SIX

Sharing Your Garden

Love Byte

You Hold the Key to Falling in Love

The final step involves celebrating the "couple self" while maintaining your individual self—in other words, maintaining boundaries. One reliable guide is to not lose sight of what gives you pleasure. In a sense we have come full circle: you began your love journey by consciously cultivating pleasure. Now, by connecting with the activities and people who give you pleasure, you maintain an environment that supports you and the love in your life.

This is the final hurdle any otherwise strong and satisfying relationship faces. In our newfound sense of shared closeness, we sometimes give up many of the activities and friends that made us individuals. As I mentioned in Step Two, it is unrealistic for either party to expect the relationship to satisfy all of his or her needs.

It's important to stress that you are not rejecting your partner by having and even developing your own interests. Both parties must maintain the delicate balance between their shared space and activities and those things each one does outside the relationship, but always being prepared to accept some give-and-take, depending on the circumstances.

— ✦ 12 ✦ —

Maintaining Boundaries:
Celebrating Your Couple Self Without
Losing Your Individual Self

Confronting the Third and Final Crossroads

The first two crossroads you faced in our love journey were the private, hidden issues about love and relationships that surfaced without warning, and our tendency to abandon our friends and other relationships in the search for love. The third crossroad you face was mentioned briefly in the previous chapter: maintaining boundaries; in other words, maintaining your sense of self.

You first fell in love because of the pleasure it gave you. Now that you have love in your life, you face the challenge of finding shared pleasures without forsaking the things that gave you pleasure in the first place. This becomes even more complicated when we factor in not just our partner but also the challenges children and other family members present to any relationship.

A relationship is like a cell—it is its own world, but it also exists in a larger world. There are many levels of interaction going on at once: the dynamic between the parts of itself and its whole, the dynamic between the whole and its environment, and the dynamic between the whole system and time and change. Love provides us with an interesting challenge: for it to work, we must be constantly aware of ourselves and our own pleasure while not losing sight of the relationship or of our partner's needs.

Again, if you are not yet in a romantic relationship, and I'm sure you will be soon, you can put these concepts to work in your friendships and other relationships.

One for All and All for One

When you become a member of a couple, one of the tasks that takes the most conscious effort is respecting and maintaining boundaries, both your own and your partner's. For example, when your home and his home become "our home," what each of you needs individually must coexist with what you need together.

Couples often make the mistake of focusing on what they need as a couple to the exclusion of their individual needs. This approach may work for a while, but sooner or later your individual needs will cry out for attention. You will have two choices when your individual needs reassert themselves: repress them (which never works for long), or negotiate them with your partner.

To do this, you must first know what it is that you need. I need order in my home, yet my nuclear family likes to spread their work out everywhere and have it remain untouched until it is complete, a process that can take days.

At first we tried designating space for each person's work, but somehow it always ended up in the living room anyway because we all like interaction as we work. I now have permission to move work to another location as long as I don't rearrange it. I, in turn, have learned to bear with unfinished projects in all corners of the apartment. (The projects would all be in the middle had I not been granted permission to move them.)

You may not like some of his friends and he may not like some of yours. You may want to work through some of your feelings without sharing them, as may he. Intuition can be used unobtrusively, so you use it to know when to respect another's privacy rather than to breach it. A relationship in which the boundaries of the members are respected is a relationship in which you will not need protection from each other, and you will not need to distance yourself from the relationship in order to experience your individuality. (I'm still working on the challenge of Super Bowl Sunday. Any suggestions would be appreciated!)

Sometimes you may feel excluded by your partner's boundaries. This is a time for discussion. You can use intuition to find a way to express your feelings such that he can respond to them without feeling devoured.

Building Intuitively Loving Couples

While intuition allows this kind of connection at times, its more important function is to keep each individual aware and respectful of the ever-shifting set of boundaries between himself and his partner. Intuition permits couples and families to be exquisitely aware of the values of each individual, accepting the differences while reaffirming the strong river of agreement that runs through them. The acceptance of diversity creates supportive connections between couples and among family members.

Allowing for Different Rhythms Within the Relationship

Intuition is very helpful in creating a rhythm of family life that addresses the preferences of all participants and serves the needs of your family. Notice the times or tasks during the day that are most stressful for your family. Then ask yourself the intuitive question: "What changes would make this more fun and efficient for all involved?"

Allow your intuition to give you information to find an answer. You will find that the solutions tend to be very simple. I suggest addressing one event at a time so that you can evaluate the response. This works for big rituals, like creating memorable holiday celebrations, and for little ones, like the moment everyone comes home tired from his or her day. It will help you organize your life to create time for what is truly important to you as a family.

For example, your partner may need to unwind by watching television after work. This may be precisely when you need time to reconnect and share your day. One solution might be to offer a relaxing foot or head massage while you tell him about your activities. After a while, this habit can become a pleasurable part of your daily life.

These little rituals of connection can be relied upon in times of need as sources of connection, intimacy, and strength. Chocolate pudding with almond slivers, my mother's answer to childhood trauma, is still what I reach for in crisis. My father and brother have an intellectual duel when they reconnect after long periods of separation. My sisters and I go straight to each other's refrigerators. My friends and I share the ritual of coffee or tea, the preparation and serving, before we settle into conversation.

Notice the rituals you have with different people. It's when these practices begin to break down that you know there's trouble in a relationship. When the long quiet hug that you usually share with your partner is forgotten, or when you're too busy to offer a cup of tea to a friend, then this often signals a time when issues need to be addressed in your relationship with that person or in your own, separate life. After all, if you're busy you could ask your friend to make the tea, and a hug only takes a moment.

Building Intuitive, Pleasurable Rituals for the Family

I often hear people around holiday time complaining of having to go visit their families. The most important intuitive question that a family can address is how to make interactions more pleasurable. There seems to be a common theme in family life of getting things done at the expense of cooperating to create a good life. I want to share with you something that I recently learned: "things" never get done, so what counts is how you do them. Each person's needs and tastes must be addressed in every interaction.

This idea is much simpler than it seems if you allow your intuition to provide solutions. For example, my five-year-old loves "chemistry experiments" but hates taking baths. One day as I was opening a kitchen cabinet, I noticed a box of baking soda. The idea flashed in my mind of giving him baking soda and vinegar (both good for his skin) in the bathtub to create a makeshift volcano.

My sister is great at explaining; I'm great at high-energy play. I don't explain new games, she doesn't go out in the snow, and our two sons each respect our limitations and love their aunts. Our household at dinner is pleasant (most of the time) because we have found a common activity that we all enjoy at the table: making up stories and telling jokes.

We often form negative family rituals without knowing it. For example, perhaps you are always awake first and end up doing the morning chores. By the time your husband gets up, you're already feeling angry and resentful. Conflicts consume a lot of energy. Change what you can, and work on ameliorating what you can't by focusing on what you can change about your own behavior to create pleasure for yourself. Finally, allow patience and understanding to create communication and opportunity for change. There's almost always a middle road.

As the needs of the individuals change, rituals mature. The goal, however, always remains the same: to focus on connection and mutual pleasure. Over time, pleasurable habits become rituals that provide nourishment and sustain connection. Whether you have two minutes or two hours in the morning, make time to connect with your family in a way that celebrates the bonds among you. My family and I have our hard times, like any other family, but our rituals provide an anchor for those eruptions and a pulse of strength throughout our family.

Intuition and Parenting

Two things struck me the moment just after my son was born. The first was how instantly and absolutely I loved this stranger who had just entered my life. The second was the sobering reality that his needs introduced into my life.

If you have a child (or children, bless their hearts), he or she is surely the single most demanding element in your life. A child's basic needs cannot wait, nor do you want them to. You also have other elements in your life—friends, spouse, work, not to mention basic body maintenance like showers—all of which require your attention, yet none of which will remind you of this fact with quite your child's volume or sense of urgency!

That said, I'd like to share with you a little trick I learned early on that has made raising Samson more pleasurable. You can raise a child by the book, or you can find a way to rear your child that you actually enjoy. For example, when my son was a baby, his basic routine was to wake up, eat, play for a while, and then go to sleep. This routine ran in three-hour cycles, twenty-four hours a day, seven days a week. At first I tried to have normal days, staying awake with him all night and then getting up in the morning to start my day. I was exhausted, and my life was totally baby-oriented.

I was lucky enough to have a great group of friends who would drop by after work and hang out or invite us to events and include Samson. Samson quickly learned to sleep in the little pack I carried him in (as long as the pack was attached to me). I really enjoyed being able to socialize and provide for Samson's needs at the same time. As Samson and I grew to know each other better, I found more and more things we both enjoyed:

- We spent days wandering through museums and discovering the city.

- We dropped in on friends at work; we walked through the parks.

- As Samson grew older, we dug through the contents of boxes after our apartment renovation.

- I continually spoke to him about the size of the building we had just passed, or the color of taxis.

- We searched the city for construction sites, and I would enjoy a hot cup of coffee on a stoop as the front loader and dump truck engaged his attention.

- I read the novels I wanted to read out loud with dramatic flair, and he listened with rapt attention.

- He brought me treasures from the ground, and together we dumped glue on paper and transformed them into art.

- I learned to sleep when he slept, and to enjoy the quiet early morning hours awake.
- I let my hair grow—who has time for haircuts?—and got plenty of exercise carrying a large baby around the city.
- I rediscovered playgrounds and children's museums.
- I also met a whole new group of friends who, like myself, had wonderful children that left them with little time for haircuts or even to bother with finding matching socks.

You can always find ways to make life enjoyable for yourself, your child, and your family if you focus on finding activities that you both enjoy. Of course, no parent can entirely avoid exhaustion, but if you focus on what you enjoy in common, what is one of the most demanding jobs in life will also become the most pleasurable. You will also find that as your child changes and grows, you will change and grow as well. This will result if you share a life as a family, instead of having your life, as it sometimes seems, taken over by the demands of your child, as joyful as those demands can be.

You'll be in conversation with a friend when your child takes his first steps away from you. You'll be better able to applaud his independence, and he'll take pride in your confidence in him. Why ruin it by telling him that you are simply basking in the fact that this is your first uninterrupted adult conversation of more than three minutes' duration since his birth? As he seeks his independence, you will have more time to reexperience yours, and you'll both be more at peace with the changes in the relationship.

Forming Communities

One of the most important gifts my family received when Samson was born was a T-shirt (far too large for Samson to wear and too small for me) that said: "A family is a circle of friends who love you."

The wisdom of this message became apparent when two uninterrupted hours of sleep while a friend watched the baby became more precious than gold, or when friends at my restaurant table began wearing napkins "bib-style" to protect their clothes from my son.

There was something to learn when I realized that Aunt Joanne's way of burping Samson (much like playing an African drum) might not be my method of choice but wouldn't kill him (he actually seemed to enjoy it). Or that Uncle Alexander's throwing him ten feet in the air would probably not cause him to hit the ceiling and shatter (although I did warn him that Samson's head might not be as firmly attached to his neck as his own).

In fact, allowing room for these relationships is probably one of the greatest gifts I have ever given my son. A love relationship of any kind is about give-and-take, about the bond between you and the person you love. But it also must be about allowing each other to be a stronger individual and to form stronger bonds with the other members of your separate families.

As Samson has grown older, he has formed a community of his own, composed of his friends, teachers, and adults he feels comfortable with. My partner has a family of his own, and I have a family of my own. Some of our community intersects and some of it does not. By allowing each other to define ourselves outside our nuclear family we allow our family to be a place of nourishment.

You'll also find that other people will entertain, discipline, feed, and handle your child in their own unique ways. Dr. June Blum, a gifted and pragmatic psychotherapist, gave me the best piece of child-rearing advice I've ever received: "Choose your battles." I carry it with me to this day in all of my relationships.

If your focus is on mutual pleasure, all of the members of your family will feel welcome. The children of my circle of friends are aware that they are a source of great pleasure and satisfaction for their parents. This knowledge allows them to interact confidently with the world. For example, I love to blend perfumes and body oils and was touched that my son actually knew me well enough to pick the perfect holiday present for me on his own. He made me a ceramic perfume bottle, painted it yellow ("I know it's your favorite color, Mommy, because it's the color of the sun, my name") and printed, in his magnificent five-year-old hand, his name on the bottom.

Families, like communities, function best when everyone feels invested and responsible. I loved my son's nursery school because they called play "work." This paradoxical renaming put the task of early childhood in perspective for both the parents and the children, giving the same respect to the child's efforts as we do to the more serious efforts of adults. Everybody has abilities and capabilities and is responsible for using them. Even a one-year-old has his work to do, which is different, of course, from the work you or I do, but is no less a part of making a successful family.

In my previous book *Practical Intuition™ for Success* I explained that work needs to have integrity for us to be successful. Integrity comes from doing not only what you feel is meaningful but also from doing what is meaningful and desirable for others. In this way, the world can feed you as in turn you feed the world. The integrity of a family comes from each individual doing his or her own work, all members contributing what they can and taking what they need. Over time, the tasks change and the roles evolve. But each family member's contribution should be acknowledged and everyone's challenges accepted with an eye toward both individual and collective growth.

Recently I overhead a friend, after being hit by her young boy, say, "We are not a family that hits." What she was really saying to her son was this: "We are a family and you are a part of this family, and this is something that our family doesn't do. I know that you are capable of not hitting because you are part of this family." We often foil our children's opportunities to be a working part of the family by insisting that they do tasks as we would do them. We sometimes do the same with our spouses. It's important to remember that an unpleasant task becomes meaningful when we bring pleasure to another by doing it, and when our contribution is acknowledged. Whatever its size, your family must be able to say, "We are a family who share our fears as well as our hopes, our joys as well as our disappointments," or whatever.

Remember to Celebrate

Can you answer these questions: What do I have in my life to be thankful for today? What did I give to myself or others that is good today? How did I celebrate life?

The other day a close friend was staying at my house for the weekend with her two children. Her nine-year-old had a homework assignment to find large numbers in books, newspapers, and magazines. We were all getting ready to go sightseeing in town and my friend asked him, "Why don't you just get this over with so you don't have to think about it?" I chimed in, "Wait, this is a great project. Let's bring the homework paper with us and wherever we go let's look for big numbers." We all found a lot of big numbers that day and had a great time doing it.

The moral of this story is that we must find a way to enjoy life's "assignments." Celebrate the moment-to-moment reality of being alive. Find toothpaste that you love (after all, you have to brush a few times a day); make sure that your purse or briefcase is comfortable to carry. If you're still looking for a lover to share your love with, find ways to enjoy the search. If you're in a relationship, find ways to enjoy your routine together. Most of all, remember to celebrate yourself.

Love starts within: chemically, unconsciously, emotionally, physically, and intuitively. If you can't perceive love within, you might have oceans of love around you and yet still experience it as empathy. You probably know at least one person with a wonderful spouse and everything anybody could want, yet who doesn't celebrate her good fortune and can't feel the grace of what she has in her life. This person should read chapter 1 and return to pleasure. This is someone out of touch with the love inside herself. When the chemicals that initially attract us and make us fall in love wear off, the unique patterns and experiences of celebration in your relationship will keep you lovingly together through good times and bad.

Checklist

-   I create pleasure and the state of love in my life every day.
-   I know how to receive intuitive information about myself and others, and how to project telepathically messages compatible with my love goal.
-   I know what I want in a love relationship, and what I am willing to offer in return.

ᨀ I take active steps each day to affirm my goal.

ᨀ I have begun to clear space in my life for love.

ᨀ I am actively repatterning my inner life, especially by confronting hidden issues I may have about love relationships.

ᨀ I am actively repatterning my outer life, examining intuitively and otherwise the ways I present myself and interact with others.

ᨀ I reaffirm my friendships and other meaningful relationships, and I continually practice my relationship skills.

ᨀ I have begun to develop a support network to help me on my love journey.

ᨀ I put my relationship skills to work in communicating with my partner (and others) and in resolving differences.

ᨀ I share and celebrate my couple self without losing touch with my individual self.

❦ *A Closing Note* ❧

I want to thank Adam Robinson and Samson Day for being the Stars and the Sun of my world, my pride and joy, and for reminding me when it's time to do laundry.

Samson would say, "I knew that already," as Samson, now six, has figured out that I don't know everything and he knows much more than he did back when he thought I knew everything. Adam would agree that "Yeah, we knew that already," having heard everything I have to say at least a dozen times by now.

So, I'm repeating myself! Those Y chromosomes. Go figure.

xxxxxxxxxxxxxxxxxxxxxxxxxxxxxxxxxxxxxxxxxxxxxxxxxxxxx

Why so many *x*s? Because with *x* and *y* together, I don't get enough *zzz*s!